PORTFOLIO of PHOTOGRAPHS

OF

FAMOUS SCENES, CITIES AND PAINTINGS

PREPARED UNDER THE SUPERVISION OF THE DISTINGUISHED
LECTURER AND TRAVELLER

JOHN L. STODDARD

CONTAINING A RARE AND ELABORATE COLLECTION OF PHOTOGRAPHIC VIEWS OF THE
ENTIRE WORLD OF NATURE AND ART

PRESENTING AND DESCRIBING THE CHOICEST TREASURES OF

EUROPE, ASIA, AFRICA, AUSTRALIA, NORTH AND SOUTH AMERICA

THE OLD WORLD AND THE NEW

———

PUBLISHED WEEKLY BY
THE WERNER COMPANY
OF CHICAGO

John L. Stoddard.

INTRODUCTION

SOME YEARS AGO, in the heart of the Rocky Mountains, a gentleman encountered a French priest, his locks completely white with age, travelling apparently for pleasure. Astonished at the sight he ventured to inquire what had induced him at his time of life to go so far from home. "'Tis very easily explained," replied the priest; "six months ago I was apparently about to die. One night I dreamed that I was already in God's presence and that he spoke to me these words: 'My child, how did you like the beautiful world I gave you to dwell in?' I answered nothing; in fact I was too mortified to answer. For think of it! I who had preached for fifty years continually of a 'better world,' had never examined this at all. Awaking from my dream I made a vow to God, that if he gave me back my health, I would devote some months at least to seeing and admiring his works. So here I am, making a tour of the world."

All of us cannot, it is true, pursue the plan of the French priest in actually travelling around the globe, but, thanks to modern art, even those whom circumstances keep at home may make that tour in imagination.

"The world is mine!" cried Monte Cristo on emerging from his dungeon. "The world is mine!" may now exclaim each man, woman and child who holds this volume in his hands, in a far truer sense than any of their ancestors could possibly have used these words even fifty years ago. Then men could only READ descriptions of the marvels of the world in nature, architecture, painting, sculpture, or imposing ruins, but had no means of looking on their counterparts save in some rare and frequently inaccurate paintings or engravings. To-day, how changed the scene! In order to make real advancement, "Hitch your wagon to a star," was the advice of Henderson; in other words, join forces with the mighty powers of the universe, and progress is assured. And man has followed the advice of that Philosopher of Concord. Some daring spirits made OUR "Star" (the sun) their willing slave, and, lo! by the assistance of that subtle alchemist the wonders of the earth are printed with infallible accuracy, and multiplied so easily that even the remotest village in Australia or America may hold within itself sun-tinted reproductions of rare scenes, to which even language does imperfect justice, just as the little wayside pool may treasure in its shallow depths the glorious reflection of a cloudless sky.

This admirable series will include such solar portraits selected from a multitude which hang within the picture-gallery of the traveller's memory. They cover almost every country on the globe, from the North Cape, which rises like a mighty sentinel to guard the coast of northern Europe from the Arctic storms, to where the ruined shrines of India and Egypt raise their sublime but mutilated forms in silent protest at the ravages of Time and Man, fanned meanwhile by the perfumed breath of tropic vegetation or shaded by the drooping fringes of the palm. Or, if we trace the progress of these pictures as they indicate the East and West, they show to us the strange peculiarities of race and clime, from the unique and fascinating civilization of Japan to the barbaric splendour of the Russian Kremlin or the enchanting beauty of the Bosphorus. Such faithful delineations of the works of God and Man are not designed to merely please the eye. To those who have not travelled they stimulate their longing for a visit either to the Old World or the New, and possibly lead them to decide to start at once and make their life-dream a reality.

To those who have been fortunate enough to see their grand originals, these pictures serve as charming souvenirs, recalling pleasant incidents which might otherwise have faded gradually from their recollection. Moreover, to those who are fond of narrating to their friends the beauty of some celebrated view, or the magnificence of some famous building, these pictures deftly supplement their eloquence, and render still more vivid and attractive their description. Nor is this all. Such glimpses of the world as here lie before us, impart an added charm to books of travel and of history. To read a printed page of Prescott's story of the Conquest of Mexico certainly gives pleasure in itself; but how that pleasure is increased for us if we can turn from time to time and see portrayed in beauty and with perfect accuracy in a series like this the City of the Montezumas, or the imposing form of the sublime volcano, Popocatapetl, which at the coming of the Spaniards was still, as its old Aztec name denotes, "The Smoking Mountain," and which the Indians looked upon as the abode of tortured spirits, whose writhings in their fiery prison-house produced the great convulsions which had marked its history! Even in reference to modern times, to merely READ of Valparaiso and Chilians conveys a very limited idea of either the city or its inhabitants, compared with that acquired by the views of those identical localities. Again, and perhaps most important of all, who can sufficiently praise the influence of faithful illustrations IN STIMULATING STUDY AND INVESTIGATION?

Pictures are keys which unlock for us many libraries. Without their charm our minds too often would not be led on to explore the FACTS of which the illustrations are the SYMBOLS. Thus, pictures of the Courts of the Alhambra inspire one to learn the history of the accomplished, fascinating race, which made that Moorish citadel a peerless specimen of Arabian art and Oriental splendour.

A view of Scott's delightful home at Abbotsford, or of fair "Ellen's Isle" floating like a medallion on the bosom of Loch Katrine, awakens a desire to read the "Lady of the Lake" and other works by the same gifted author; while by beholding in reality or on the illumined page the stately Trossachs, or romantic Melrose Abbey, hallowed by Scott's genius, we realize as never before the debt of gratitude the world still owes to that enchanting "Wizard of the North." To one, therefore, who looks aright through these attractive pages the graceful forms depicted here are eloquent in their suggestiveness. A hundred different works of poetry, art, history, and fiction, by the best writers of the world, are quickly called to mind by one who sees beneath the surface of these lights and shadows. Is it on scenes in France or Germany that we are gazing? What histories of the French Revolution, of Napoleon and of Frederick the Great, do not at once present themselves as pleasurable subjects for a winter's reading? Are we beholding views of Florence? Instinctively we wish to read among the many books associated with that city of the Renaissance, George Eliot's "Romola," and Grimm's "Life of Michael Angelo." Are we enjoying Roman pictures? Here truly the amount of ecclesiastical, historical, poetical, and classic literature thus suggested is too immense to be enumerated. While hardly can a single portraiture of art or scenery in Italy, Switzerland, Greece, or on the castle-bordered Rhine, be spread out before us, without invoking memories of that incomparable volume of the traveller's library, Lord Byron's masterpiece, "Childe Harold," whose thrilling stanzas one by one were left by him like a long line of detached pearls to mark the poet's pilgrimage from land to land. For let us not deceive ourselves. THE BENEFIT OF TRAVEL COMES NOT FROM THE DISTANCE TRAVERSED NOR FROM THE SCENES REFLECTED ON THE RETINA, BUT FROM THE INTELLECTUAL STIMULUS THUS AWAKENED, AND THE AMOUNT OF THOUGHT AND READING WHICH RESULT THEREFROM, just as a man is nourished not by the quantity of food which he may EAT, but by the amount which he ASSIMILATES AND MAKES HIS OWN. Thus properly followed up and utilized, this series of selections from the world's great treasure-house may prove more beneficial to the thoughtful reader and observer than actual travel around the globe would be to one who did not wake to the significance of what he saw. "That stick, Sir, has been round the world," exclaimed a man one day to Sidney Smith, as he held out to him a valued cane. "Dear me," was the reply, "and yet it is only a stick after all." When Italy, Greece, Egypt, India, and other lands, have become PERMANENT AND INTELLIGIBLE POSSESSIONS OF OUR MINDS, then we have really in the best sense visited them. Yet one may do this by reading and the aid of illustrations even at his fireside, while some one else, apparently more fortunate, may see those countries with his own eyes and yet know next to nothing of the part which they have played on the stage of history.

An ancient proverb says that the world is a kind of a book, of which we have read merely the first page when we have seen only our own country. It is true. Goethe has justly said: "Wem Gott will rechte Kunst erweisen, Den schikt Er in die Weite Welt" ("Him whom the Gods true art would teach, They send out in the mighty world"). Whether this "sending out" into the world be interpreted literally, or as referring to the mind awakened to activity through the printed and the pictured page, the truth is still the same. Expansion, growth, broader experience, and wider charity, these are the fruits of that REAL travel which is of the MIND.

It may be said that these illustrations here are not harmonious because collected in so many and such different lands. They do present a great variety, it is true, yet the same solar artist sketched them all, as one by one the globe of which they form a part rolled its successive groups of Nature and Humanity within its brilliant grasp! To represent them all would be impossible. This series therefore may be likened to some of those mosaic tables which we occasionally see in some of the grand palaces of Florence, whose polished surface is composed of precious stones, each worthy of minute inspection, yet forming with the rest a combination of artistic excellence all the more pleasing from its wonderful variety. And if you ask what rule the lapidary has followed in his grouping of the greater part of the mosaics represented in this work, he can reply that his chief motive in selecting them has been like that of the Duke of Buckingham, when, in the place where Anne of Austria had whispered that she loved him, he purposely let fall a precious gem, desirous that by finding it another might be happy where he himself had been.

John L. Stoddard.

PANORAMA OF PARIS.—Paris is the city of the Present, as Rome is of the Past. Others may imitate it, but no metropolis of modern times can really be compared to the French capital for its elegance of decoration, the refined gaiety of its manners, and the superb arrangement of its streets and boulevards, together with the magnificence of its architectural triumphs. If Switzerland is "the play-ground of Europe," Paris is its favourite place of amusement. Hither come yearly hundreds of thousands of pleasure-seekers from every quarter of our globe. There is everything in Paris to please, instruct and charm. Almost every window is an exhibition of art. Each prominent street is frequently the centre of some Carnival. The river Seine which divides Paris into two very nearly equal sections shoots arrow-like beneath twenty-eight bridges, many of which are eloquent of history. This French metropolis has a population of nearly two and a half millions, but is exceedingly compact on account of the French custom of living in apartments rather than in separate houses. It is a beautifully *clean* city. The care bestowed upon its thoroughfares is something which excites the admiration of all tourists, and is in painful contrast to the way in which the streets of many of our great American cities are neglected. Perhaps this is one out of many reasons why "Good Americans, when they die, go to Paris."

ANN HATHAWAY'S COTTAGE, STRATFORD-ON-AVON, ENGLAND.—This charming little cottage still stands in substantially the same condition as when Shakespeare came here to whisper to his future wife, Ann Hathaway, the story of his love. It is still occupied by a descendant of the Hathaway family. There can be little doubt that the man who has given to the world that most adorable of lovers, Romeo, must have himself been an incomparable suitor. For whatever may be said about great geniuses making poor husbands, there can be little question of their fascination in those delightful moments of uncertainty and novelty commonly known as courtship and the honeymoon. Standing here listening to the nightingales and thrushes, one recalls with pleasure these lines attributed to Shakespeare:

"Would ye be taught, ye feathered throng,
　With love's sweet notes to frame your song?
　To pierce my heart with thrilling lay,
　Listen to my Ann Hathaway!
　She hath-a-way to sing so clear,
　Phœbus might, wondering, stoop to hear;

To melt the sad, make blithe the gay,
To charm all hearts, Ann hath-a-way;
　She hath-a-way,
　Ann Hathaway,
To breathe delight, Ann hath-a-way!"

ELLEN'S ISLE, LOCH KATRINE, SCOTLAND.—One of the loveliest features in the Trossachs is the little sheet of water known as Loch Katrine. It is diminutive, but so incomparably situated that its small size makes it the more enchanting, since not a single charm escapes us. What can be more attractive than the combination here of light and shade, when its fair surface is flecked by touches of the sun and clouds? Around it mountains rear their massive forms like giant guardians of the peaceful lake, within which they again appear like an inverted world, until we can with difficulty tell which is the real and which the counterfeit presentment! Moreover, its heathery banks and limpid waves, so long as they endure, will be fondly associated with memories of Sir Walter Scott and his fairest creation, the "Lady of the Lake." In fact the pretty island in the centre is still known as "Ellen's Isle," for, according to Scott's fancy, this wave-encircled sylvan retreat was the home of that fair Lady of the Lake, "Her head thrown back, her lips apart, Like Monument of Grecian art." Scott is the special genius of this place, and here one fairly revels in the scenes portrayed with absolute perfection by his magic pen. Each point recalls some stanza or some well-known line, so accurate are his poetical descriptions. Never was a writer more particular in this respect than Scott. For example, while writing the "Lady of the Lake," he once galloped the entire distance from Loch Achray to Stirling to prove to himself that his hero could have ridden it in a certain time!

BLARNEY CASTLE, IRELAND.—The "Emerald Isle" abounds in lovely bits of scenery, of which some ivy-mantled abbey or historic castle forms a charming feature. One of the most renowned of these old Irish ruins is Blarney Castle, not far from Cork. On the highest point of the northeast angle of the tower is a stone bearing the date of 1703, and held in position by two iron bars. In 1825 Sir Walter Scott, while on a tour through Ireland, kissed this "Blarney Stone," as thousands of tourists do every year. The effect which this act has upon the eloquence of anyone who thus salutes it is thus told in verse:

"There is a stone there
That whoever kisses
Oh! he never misses
    To grow eloquent.
'Tis he may clamber

To a lady's chamber
Or become a member
    Of Parliament.
A clever spouter
He'll sure turn out, or
An out-and-outer

To be left alone.
    Don't hope to hinder him,
    Or to bewilder him;
    Sure, he's a pilgrim
From the Blarney Stone."

PANORAMA OF STOCKHOLM, SWEDEN.—Stockholm is one of the most beautifully located cities in the world. It has been called the Venice of the North. It is founded on six islands, and through it sweeps a glorious flood of deep green water, which is the overflow of the beautiful Lake Malar, half a mile away, making its tumultuous exit to the Baltic. How fascinating is that mass of emerald water rushing impetuously through the city with half the uproar of a cataract! Upon its fair expanse, a stone's throw only from the Grand Hotel, are usually half a dozen steamers bound to various places on the Swedish coast, while through their midst, from point to point, dart back and forth a multitude of little steam launches, about the size of tug-boats. These are the ferry-boats of Stockholm, and take the place of horse cars in our cities. On some of the islands of Stockholm, and at many points in its vicinity, are lovely gardens and places of amusement, which make the Swedish capital a charming place of residence in summer. The people then spend as much time as possible in the open air. There is then in that northern latitude almost no darkness, and the long summer evenings, marked by a silvery light that never wanes, but merely brightens into dawn, are even more enchanting than the days. The cordial hospitality, sunny disposition and exquisite politeness of the Swedes are additional reasons why the traveller remembers Stockholm with great pleasure.

GROUP OF LAPPS, NORWAY.—Near the North Cape, on the northwestern coast of Norway, are settlements of Laplanders, frequently visited by travellers in their tour through the "Land of the Midnight Sun." One visit usually satisfies the tourist's curiosity. The Lapps are by no means beautiful, attractive or cleanly. They are short in stature, the men being about five feet high, and the women four. They usually have high cheek bones, wizened faces, flat noses, and small almond-shaped eyes. They wear garments made of reindeer skin with the pelt turned outwards. These garments last indefinitely and are handed down from parents to children. The lower limbs of the Lapps are usually covered with bands of worsted wound about the ankles, and leggins of whale skin, which fit their forms almost as tightly as if they were their own skin. The Lapps live in miserable huts made of wood, turf and straw, and lined with reindeer hide. One of these will often contain two or three families. They sell to tourists bone knives, fur purses and other objects of their own manufacture. They are tough and hardy like most dwarfs, and Dickens could have found among them many models for his character of Quilp. They are great smokers, and, as their huts are also filled with smoke, they apparently become at last thoroughly smoke-dried within and without. This creates an ardent thirst, and they are in consequence very fond of intoxicating liquors. When a Norwegian wishes to remonstrate with a friend for drinking to excess, he will say to him : "Don't make a Lapp of yourself."

HEIDELBERG CASTLE, GERMANY.—One of the most charming features of the Old World is Heidelberg Castle towering above the river Neckar, which rolls beneath it like a flood of silver to the Rhine not many miles away. · Its situation is glorious. From the "Castle Hotel," just above the ruin itself, one gazes with increasing pleasure upon the shadow-darkened river and the great forest all about him, like a magnificent rug of deepest green, from which the castle rises in its grandeur. The forest itself is threaded with countless paths completely sheltered from the sun, in early spring-time lined with violets and spanned at frequent intervals by half-ruined arches, crowned with luxuriant wild flowers and caressed by the clinging fingers of a hundred vines. A great variety of architecture is here displayed. Each portion of the building differs in style and finish from its neighbour. The roofs possess no similarity. The great round tower is unique. But after a moment's thought this difference in style is understood. For Heidelberg Castle was not, after all, the work of any *one* great architect, or even *one age*, but rather is a series of old palaces erected here by various princes through 300 years. A wonderfully fascinating place is the old court of Heidelberg either just after sunset, or better still when the full moon is threading its deserted courts with silver sandals. In that mysterious light its sculptured kings and warriors seem like living beings gathered here to speak of the old times when these grand halls were filled with valiant knights, fair ladies and sweet-voiced minstrels.

LUCERNE, SWITZERLAND.—One of the best known gateways into Switzerland is Lucerne, which greets us ever with a smile, peacefully resting by its lovely lake. How many travellers will testify to the charm and beauty of this place, where one stands full of expectation, on the threshold of the land of mountains. It is a curious old town. Its pretty river is crossed by ancient bridges, adorned with quaint old paintings, and guarded still by mediæval towers, which seem a trifle out of place within a land whose natural ramparts have been reared by the Almighty, and rise to such immensity that *man's* poor battlements look in comparison like children's toys. One of these sentinels, which almosts casts its shadow on the town itself, is Mt. Pilate, 7,000 feet in height, harsh, cold and uninviting in appearance, yet in reality containing thirty "Alps" or mountain meadows, upon which graze four or five thousand head of sheep and cattle. Upon this mountain Pontius Pilate is said to have committed suicide in his remorse for his condemnation of Jesus. But Mt. Pilate has a dangerous rival here; for on the other side of the old town is that most fashionable Alpine peak, the *Righi*. Both of them now are easy to ascend, for enterprise has girded their steep sides with iron rails, drawn paths of steel through their black-bearded forests, and finally has placed upon their crests a number of hotels. Moreover, in front of Lucerne is its enchanting lake, twenty-two miles in length, along which steamers glide continuously, their shaded decks containing hundreds of delighted tourists.

THE GRABEN, VIENNA.—One of the oldest and most interesting streets in Vienna is that which we may now in imagination enter, called the *Graben*. It derives its name from **the fact** that this was the ancient *Grab*, or moat surrounded by the fortified wall, which rose where now are yonder buildings containing some of the most luxurious and expensive retail shops **in** Vienna. One would hardly expect to find within this busy street the solitary survivor of the famous Wiener Wald, the ancient forest bordering the Danube! Yet at one corner of it is a **most** extraordinary looking object, protected partly by the wall of the building, and partly by some bands of iron. It is the famous *Stock im Eisen*, or the *Iron stick*. It is well named, **for its** appearance is precisely that of an iron club. Investigation, however, proves it to be a mass of wood, literally covered with nails, to some of which coins are attached. One of these has **the** date of 1575. This ancient tree, (which apparently could not crumble now if it should try to) was for some cause, now unknown, esteemed especially sacred; and every one who drove **a nail** into its precious wood, received a spiritual shield against the devil. How odd it seems to see this strange reminder of the past, standing thus grimly in the very centre of the city's life! **Just** as some superstition, like a dread of Friday or thirteen at a table, still exists amid the common sense and science of the nineteenth century.

"THE DYING GAUL," CAPITOL, ROME.—One of the best known and most justly admired statues which have come down to us from antiquity is this pathetic figure popularly called the "Dying Gladiator," but probably representing a dying Gaul. In any case no words which have ever been written in regard to it are so appropriate and eloquent as the immortal lines of Byron:

" I see before me the Gladiator lie ;
    He leans upon his hand—his manly brow
Consents to death, but conquers agony,
    And his droop'd head sinks gradually low—
    And through his side the last drops, ebbing slow
From the red gash, fall heavy, one by one,
    Like the first of a thunder-shower ; and now
The Arena swims around him—he is gone,
    Ere ceased the inhuman shout which hailed the wretch who won.

" He heard it, but he heeded not—his eyes
    Were with his heart, and that was far away ;
He reck'd not of the life he lost nor prize,
    But where his rude hut by the Danube lay,
    There were his young barbarians all at play,
There was their Dacian mother—he, their sire,
    Butcher'd to make a Roman holiday—
All this rush'd with his blood—Shall he expire ?
    And unavenged ? Arise ! ye Goths, and glut your ire !"

STATUE OF COLUMBUS, GENOA, ITALY.—"Genoa la Superba" well deserves its name.   Its situation is glorious and the view of the ocean spread out beneath its flower-crowned terraces is magnificent.   The history of this city is brilliant and eventful, and one ever memorable feature of it is commemorated in this noble statue recently erected in a prominent square directly in front of the principal Genoese railway station.   It greets the traveller, therefore, on arriving here ; it bids him farewell as he takes his leave.   The inscription briefly tells us what this handsome monument signifies, viz: The gift of a grateful country to Christopher Columbus.   For it is the glory of Genoa to have been in 1435 the birthplace of that immortal discoverer. What though it has been proved that hardy Norsemen crossed the North Atlantic centuries before Columbus sailed from Spain? His courage, faith and perseverance are not less sublime. Whatever Northern Vikings may have done, America was still in 1492 virtually a *terra incognita*, and it was the illustrious son of Genoa who brought it to the knowledge of the civilized world and revolutionized the ideas, hopes and destinies of mankind.   The design of this monument is admirable.   Columbus leans upon an anchor, his right hand pointing to the figure of America.   Below him we discern, encircling the shaft, a line of naval ornaments symbolic of the discoverer's little fleet.   On the corners of the pedestal are statues representing Science, Religion, Courage and Geography, and between them scenes of his adventurous career.

THE MILAN CATHEDRAL, ITALY.—No matter how weary one may have become from visiting numberless cathedrals through the length and breadth of Europe, here is one before which he feels inclined to kneel in admiration. It is one of the most majestic, and at the same time beautiful and elaborate, structures in the world. It reveals Gothic architecture carried to its most exquisite limits. Its material is white marble. There are times, especially by moonlight, when it seems like a mountain of alabaster peopled with thousands of graceful figures. This is hardly an exaggeration, for there are actually more than 4,800 marble statues on the exterior of this marvellous structure. Nor are these figures roughly finished on account of their elevation from the street. If we ascend to the roof and examine some of them, we shall find each one an admirable work of art. Some of them are the products of Canova's genius. To walk over the roof of this "eighth wonder of the world" is to wander through aerial sculpture-galleries, surrounded by myriads of columns, towers, pinnacles, buttresses and arches, all tenanted by snow-white angels, warriors, saints, kings or cherubs, outlined at times like frosted silver on the sky. It should be also remembered that the interior of this marble Duomo is worthy of the exterior in the grandeur of its dimensions, its gigantic fluted columns, and its magnificent stained glass windows, through which the rays of sunlight fall on the vast mosaic pavement like the ruby and golden hues of autumnal leaves.

THE GARDEN OF GETHSEMANE, PALESTINE.—At the base of the Mount of Olives is a small enclosure surrounded by a white-washed wall. It is the reputed Garden of Gethsemane. The Franciscan monks possess it and admit all visitors to it with courtesy. There are now seven venerable olive trees in the enclosure, whose gnarled and aged trunks give proof of their great antiquity. They are indeed said to be the very ones under which Jesus knelt in spiritual anguish. This can hardly be the case, for the Romans are said to have cut down all the trees about Jerusalem, and the Crusaders stated that the valley was destitute of wood. Nevertheless since it is a fact that the olive tree springs repeatedly from the same root, there is a possibility that these trees are the descendants of those which sheltered the Man of Sorrows. Around the Garden are several shrines for prayer, and the exact places are pointed out where Jesus was arrested, where Judas gave to his Master the fatal kiss and where Peter, James and John slept while their Saviour prayed. The earliest account of this Garden dates from the fourth century. There is no doubt that its situation corresponds closely to that which the nature of the ground makes evidently necessary. But whether it be the *precise* locality is questionable. The Greeks have their Garden of Gethsemane at a little distance from this, and they maintain that theirs is the only genuine one. Certain it is, however, that somewhere in a very limited area here the scenes of the Agony, Betrayal and Arrest must have occurred.

BOTANICAL GARDENS AND MT. CORCOVADO, RIO DE JANEIRO, BRAZIL.—Just outside the city limits is a park of which all Brazilians are justly proud. The Botanical Gardens of Rio are indeed famed throughout the world, one particularly lovely feature of them being a long, straight avenue of majestic palm trees. The vegetation around the city is, in almost any direction, so luxuriant and beautiful that one writer has declared that the bay of Rio is "the gate to a tropical paradise." The road leading to this Botanical Park is nothing but a continuous garden in itself. Here almost every variety of tropical fruit abounds, and flowers of rare beauty fill the air with a delicious fragrance. Close by this is Mount Corcovado, three thousand feet in height, on which there is a copious spring of clear, cold water. This is the principal water supply of the Brazilian capital, and the precious liquid is conveyed to the reservoirs and numerous fountains of the city by means of an aqueduct, built more than a century ago. It is twelve miles long, and crosses a valley ninety feet deep on two great tiers of arches. If a citizen of Rio were asked which he considered the two most charming features of his city, he would probably reply: "The view of our incomparable Bay, and our magnificent Botanical Gardens."

BOULEVARD DE LA MADELEINE, PARIS.—Beginning at the noble church of the Madeleine, which so forcibly resembles a Greek Temple, there extends for nearly three miles to the Place de la Bastille a series of beautiful thoroughfares known as THE original Paris Boulevards par excellence. There are eleven of these streets, succeeding one another like links in a golden chain. The first is the one outlined in this representation, and is called (from the building at its commencement) the Boulevard de la Madeleine. There is a charm about these Boulevards which no other streets in the world seem to possess. They are a recognized rendezvous for fashionable idlers and pleasure-seekers. Throngs of elegant vehicles pass and repass here every afternoon in bewildering succession. On their broad sidewalks there are not simply thousands of promenaders, but hundreds of men and women seated at little tables in front of glittering cafés, sipping coffee or eau sucrée, or eating an ice-cream, as an excuse to have the privilege of occupying, as it were, an orchestra chair or proscenium box at this attractive spectacle of life and gaiety, of which the Boulevard itself is the stage. And if this be true of the Boulevards in the *afternoon*, still more brilliant and animated do these sidewalks become on pleasant *evenings*, when every café is radiant with lights repeated in innumerable mirrors, and when every jeweller's windows look like the entrance to Aladdin's fabled cavern! Two features of Parisian Boulevards will be recalled by every traveller. They are the tall, circular structures called "Kiosques," some of which are merely covered with theatrical advertisements, while others serve as newspaper stands, or little bars for the sale of unintoxicating drinks.

2

WESTMINSTER ABBEY, LONDON.—If only one object in London could be selected for inspection by American tourists, it would doubtless be Westminster Abbey. The original church was erected here about the year 610, but this and two successors were pulled down and rebuilt, till finally this present Abbey was constructed in the reign of Henry III. It is in the form of a Latin cross four hundred feet in length. Although impressive and in places beautiful, its Gothic exterior will not account for the fascination which this building exerts upon the visitor. That is unquestionably due to the fact that for so many centuries it has been the English Pantheon, the burial place of kings and queens, statesmen, generals, explorers, orators, philosophers and literary geniuses. Thirteen English Kings and fourteen Queens are here entombed. Here also is preserved, as every visitor may see, the ancient chair in which all English sovereigns have been crowned (and most of them in this Cathedral) since Edward I. Here are the tombs of Queen Elizabeth and her fair rival and victim, Mary Queen of Scots, now lying 'neath the same Cathedral roof. The one apparently completely triumphed and saw the body of her hated cousin entombed within an unpretending sepulchre! But posterity has been more just. The murdered Mary's son ascended England's throne, and Mary's tomb was placed beside Elizabeth's in England's noblest shrine; and not a day goes by, or *has* gone by for centuries, but pilgrims to Westminster stand beside their graves and sigh in pity for the one, and blame the conduct of the other!

SACKVILLE STREET, DUBLIN.—The Irish are exceedingly proud of their capital, and well they may be. Its situation on the river Liffey near its entrance into Dublin Bay is beautiful, and many of its public buildings command the traveller's admiration. Its principal thoroughfare, Sackville Street, has few superiors in Europe. In the centre, and dividing it into upper and lower Sackville Street, is a fluted Doric column 134 feet in height, crowned by the statue of Nelson, and reared to commemorate the hero of Trafalgar. The cost of the monument was about £7,000, which was raised by popular subscription. On every anniversary of Nelson's greatest victories the Union Jack is displayed from the top of the column. But the Nelson Monument is only one of the many striking features of Sackville Street. Here, for example, is the General Post Office, presenting a long and handsome facade adorned with statuary. Here also are several statues of distinguished Irish patriots, and many of the finest business blocks and hotels of the city. Moreover, this is the great promenade of Dublin, and it has been often stated that nowhere can there be seen more beautiful women than one may meet here on a pleasant afternoon. For if a "real old Irish gentleman" is one of the most agreeable of acquaintances and one of the truest and warmest of friends, so Irish ladies are not only charming in form and feature, but remarkably attractive from the rare combination they exhibit of high breeding and dignity together with a quick sympathy and warm-hearted impulsiveness, which no mere covering of conventionality can ever quite conceal.

CASINO, MONTE CARLO, ITALY.—One of the loveliest places on the curving shore of the Mediterranean is the famous gambling resort of Monte Carlo. It is laid out in cultivated terraces, which overhang the pretty bay, where a multitude of pleasure boats are always moored. So far as outward attractiveness is concerned, Nature and Art have here combined to make this spot a veritable bit of paradise. Before it is the boundless sea, as smooth as glass and many coloured as a prism; while in the rear are lovely olive-coloured mountains which at sunset invariably fold about their dimpled shoulders mantles of royal purple. Around this Casino, aloes and orange trees are growing in luxuriance, and here and there a tufted palm outlines its graceful form against the cloudless sky. Monte Carlo owes much of its attractiveness to the late M. Blanc, who founded here this handsome gaming house. At present the establishment is in the hands of a French Company, and constantly entices weak humanity thither by its glittering promises of wealth. Within this Casino, apart from the gaming halls, there are well-furnished reading-rooms, and a richly decorated theatre, where one can often hear delightful music. Russians are said to squander the most money here, but France furnishes the greatest number of players. Germans also are quite numerous, but usually play with caution. England and America too are represented here, but chiefly by spectators rather than participants in the alluring game. From twelve to fifteen suicides occur here nearly every month.

EDINBURGH, AND SCOTT'S MONUMENT.—Not another capital in Europe save Athens, which it somewhat resembles, compares with Edinburgh in situation, and the Scotch have made the place well worthy of its fine position. On one side is Calton Hill, rising three hundred feet above the town, and opposite this, about a mile away, is the old historic Castle. Between them extends the beautiful avenue called Princes Street, bordered by handsome buildings, parks and monuments. Among the many attractive sights in this old Scottish city, and rising in the centre of this picture, is the elegant memorial of Sir Walter Scott, who was born in Edinburgh on the 15th day of August, 1771. The statues in its various niches represent characters taken from his works, such as Meg Merrilees, the Last Minstrel, and the Lady of the Lake. In the centre, open on all sides to inspection, is a colossal marble statue of Sir Walter, and at the feet of one so fond of dogs is appropriately placed the figure of his favourite hound Maida. This monument is certainly one of the finest ever reared to a man of genius. Its graceful arches recall in miniature the groined roofs of Melrose Abbey. All parts of it are beautifully carved. A stairway of about 280 steps leads to the top. The cost of this great work was about £16,000, and its design was furnished by a young architect of Edinburgh, who did not live to see the monument completed. It is a touching proof of the love which Scotland felt for Sir Walter, that subscriptions for this grand memorial poured in from all classes and conditions of his countrymen. It was the gift of a Nation; and while on the subscription list may be seen "100 Pounds from Her Majesty the Queen," we may likewise read, "Three pounds seven shillings from the poor people of the Cowgate."

NORTH CAPE, NORWAY.—Travel in Norway naturally divides itself in three sections; first, the drive through its mountainous interior; second, the exploration of its grand Fjords; and third, the voyage from Trondjhem to the North Cape. This voyage in the fast excursion steamers, which run two or three times a week during the summer months, occupies eight days for the round trip. It is a charming expedition, for only in a few places need rough weather be feared, since for almost the entire distance the steamer glides along in smooth water between the coast of Norway and the long fringe of islands which serve for more than 1,000 miles as a break-water to protect the Norwegian shore from the billows of the North Atlantic. The North Cape is a most imposing promontory rising with gloomy almost perpendicular cliffs from the dark ocean at its base. It is in reality an island, stationed like a gigantic sentinel a little in advance, as if to guard the coast of Europe from the Arctic's storms. The ascent is not dangerous, but very wearisome. On the summit a small granite monument has been erected to commemorate King Oscar's visit to the Cape in 1873. Just before midnight rockets are fired from the steamer to warn such passengers as may then find themselves on the mountain to be on their guard. It is a never-to-be-forgotten moment when one stands upon this northern boundary of Europe, so near to, yet so far from, the North Pole. And it is a unique and ever memorable experience when, as the hands of his watch point to twelve o'clock, the traveller gazes northward over the curving shoulder of the globe, and sees *the Midnight Sun!* This wonderful phenomenon of an endless day, with a brilliant sun at midnight, is visible from May 11th to July 30th; but practically for a much longer time in northern Norway there is no perceptible difference between night and day.

FRANKFORT, GERMANY.—Frankfort-on-the-Main is one of those cities which combine the characteristics of mediæval and modern Germany. Some of its streets are as winding and as narrow as they were six centuries ago, and others bear the stamp of the New Empire, broad, well paved and adorned with handsome structures. It has many interesting relics of the past. Here is the Council-House where the German Emperors were elected and entertained in the Kaisersaal, the walls of which are covered with their portraits. In its cathedral, whose spire rises far above the town, the German Emperors were crowned. Here may be seen the house in which originated the famous family of the Rothschilds. Its highest literary distinction is the fact that here the poet Gœthe was born in 1749, at No. 23 Hirschgraben. In 1863 the house was purchased for 56,000 florins, by a German society designed to promote art, science and general culture. Thus Gœthe's birthplace was made forever the common property of all German people. Its various rooms are kept as little museums of Gœthe literature and art. Near this river Main is a spot known as "Gœthe's Rest," because he is said to have there admired the situation and beauty of his native city. One square of Frankfort is also called Gœthe Platz, and is adorned with a fine bronze statue of the illustrious author of "Faust." This is a city of immense wealth, and offers a good market for American securities. Its name is said to be derived from an episode in the life of Charlemagne, when he, together with his army of *Franks*, found here a ford across the river.

ST. GOTTHARD PASS AND BRIDGE, SWITZERLAND.—The king of Alpine routes from Switzerland to Italy is the St. Gotthard.   It is impossible to speak too highly of this noble road.   Scaling the loftiest cliffs, spanning the wildest torrents, and winding through the deepest gorges, it seems like a gigantic chain, which man, the Victor, has imposed upon the vanquished Alps ; the first end guarded by the Lion of Lucerne, the last sunk deep in the Italian lakes, but all the intervening links kept gilded brightly by the hand of trade ! It is a splendid instance of the way in which these roads are made to thwart at every turn the sudden fury of the avalanche or mountain torrent.   For where experience proves a place to be unusually exposed, a solid roof extends to break the fall of rocks and ice.   Still, in these days of steam and telegraph, even this mode of travel in the Alps appears too slow for those who journey here for business purposes, and one of the most important works of this or any age is the tunnel of St. Gotthard.   This perforates yonder chain of mountains for a distance of nine and one-half miles, yet is sufficiently wide for two railway trains to run abreast. What labour must have been expended here by myriads of men, who most of the time were thousands of feet beneath the mountains, yet who at last, by the perfection of engineering skill, met and shook hands through the narrow aperture which they had pierced from the opposite sides of Switzerland and Italy !

THE VATICAN LIBRARY, ROME.—The world owes much to the enlightened and art-loving Popes who have made the Vatican not merely the abode of the Pontiff of the Catholic Church, but a wonderful treasure-house of art, where are preserved many of the grandest statues of antiquity and some of the finest paintings of the Renaissance. Moreover, its library is one of the most valuable in the world, and makes upon the traveller's mind a profound impression. The Grand Hall is no less than two hundred and forty feet in length and fifty-two in breadth. The pavement is of marble mosaic, the ceilings are resplendent with elaborate frescoes, and everywhere we see magnificent presents given by royal admirers to various Popes. Among these are vases of porphyry, urns of malachite, gold crosses, and solid silver candelabra. But these are merely external decorations for the hidden treasures of this library. Here are about 24,000 manuscripts of inestimable value, some of them being the earliest copies which we have of the Gospels. Besides these there are more than 50,000 printed books. The manuscripts and rarer volumes are not often exposed to view, but are contained within beautifully decorated cases. Among the scholars of the world who have often consulted the archives of this Vatican Library is Pope Leo XIII., whose accomplishments and tastes are highly literary. His letters and addresses are framed in most elegant and polished Latin, while verses which he writes from time to time in Latin or Italian have earned for him the title of a poet.

VIEW OF THE ALHAMBRA (FROM THE GENERALIFFE), GRANADA, SPAIN.—"The view from the Alhambra hill is, in my opinion, the most beautiful that I have ever seen, and when combined with the historic, romantic and literary associations of the place, it renders this Granadan Acropolis unequalled in attractiveness by any portion of the world." Such is the expressed opinion of a great traveller, who has had the opportunity of making extensive observations and comparisons. But his enthusiasm is not misplaced. Here is a noble plain containing fifty-seven square miles of wonderful fertility, green as the richest moss and ornamented here and there, like Oriental pearls, with white-walled villages and towers. Every portion of that plain has been the scene of desperate conflict between Moor and Christian. Around it are many mountains, only a few of which are visible on the side represented by this illustration. Some of these are tawny and desolate, while others pierce the azure at a height of 11,000 feet and are crowned with everlasting snow. With such an environment there rises abruptly above the city of Granada the hill which constituted the favourite abode of the Moorish Caliphs. It is sheltered from the arrows of the sun by magnificent elms a hundred feet in height. Nightingales are singing in their abundant foliage. Roses and orange-blossoms fill the air with perfume. Lastly and chiefly, seated here in this bower of Oriental delights, and resembling a Queen upon a lofty throne, is the most exquisite palace man has ever built, the unique, the world-renowned *Alhambra*. This, as all the world knows, was the most treasured residence of the Moorish sovereigns, a veritable earthly paradise, where life passed away like a happy dream.

THE KREMLIN, MOSCOW.—The Holy City of Russia lies in the form of two circles, one within the other. Both are surrounded by walls of fortification, and both represent successive periods of Moscow's growth. The inner circle, or core, of the Czar's capital is the far-famed *Kremlin* of Moscow. It is a citadel, or fortified enclosure containing the Imperial Palace, the Treasury, the Arsenal and many of the most revered and ancient temples in the empire. Their lofty spires and gilded domes produce a wonderful effect, enhanced by the vivid colours of their roofs, cupolas and walls, which form a glittering expanse of red, white, green, gold and silver. Originally this Kremlin, like the Acropolis of Athens, was surrounded by stout walls of oak, and in the centre of this strong enclosure lived the Czar, surrounded by his relatives and nobles. More than 500 years ago, however, the wooden walls gave place to stone ones, in order that the Tartars might be more successfully resisted. Again and again, under successive shocks of war, have those old ramparts been injured and rebuilt; but in form they have always remained substantially the same. You can hardly imagine anything more picturesque and suggestive of past conflicts with barbarians than this grand, massive and formerly impregnable circuit of the Kremlin, with parapets sixty feet in height, all loop-holed for the discharge of weapons at the advancing foe, and with its watch-towers rising thus at frequent intervals.

THE EZBEKIYEH AND STREET SCENE, CAIRO, EGYPT.—The Ezbekiyeh is an enormous square in Cairo, named after a brave Egyptian general who served under one of the last of the independent Mameluke sovereigns of Egypt in the last part of the fifteenth century. In the centre of this open space are beautiful pleasure grounds covering an area of twenty acres, and abounding in luxuriant semi-tropical vegetation. Around these are some of the finest modern edifices in Cairo, including hotels, cafés, theatres, handsome shops and residences of wealthy foreigners. During the winter an Egyptian band plays in this square for three hours every afternoon. On Sunday and Friday evenings (the Christian and the Moslem Sabbaths) the gardens here are illuminated with thousands of gas-lights and the effect is charming. Formerly only Europeans seemed to frequent the park of the Ezbekiyeh, but of late years the Arabs are beginning to send their wives and daughters here (of course suitably veiled) to enjoy the music and the flowers. This garden is another proof of how the recent Khedives of Egypt have made of Cairo a delightful winter-resort. The streets in the foreign quarter are broad, smooth and clean. They are also lighted by gas, and the hotels in Cairo are well kept and comfortable. Yet within five minutes' walk from any such surroundings one may plunge into square miles of Arabic mosques, dwellings and bazars, where he is apparently one thousand miles removed from all that would suggest European civilization. This combination of the Orient and the Occident; this blending of modern comforts with the stupendous souvenirs of an almost inconceivably remote antiquity, make Egypt at once the most mysterious and fascinating country on our globe.

CAMP OF A CARAVAN ON THE SAHARA DESERT.—Few travellers in the East venture out upon the Desert, and yet it is neither difficult nor dangerous to do so within a reasonable distance of either Algeria, Egypt or Palestine. In any case the experience is unique and can never be forgotten. You are there at once transported back to the days of the Patriarchs. You are a nomad, a Bedouin, a voyager on a petrified ocean which with its rolling waves of sand seems to have been suddenly changed from a state of activity to one of eternal rest. By day a journey on the desert means a perpetual struggle with the sun, whose heat reflected from the yellow sand seems almost unendurable. But at night the fascination of the desert's silence, solitude and awful sense of isolation 'neath the sparkling stars is something which can hardly be imagined until actually experienced. A veritable ocean the mighty desert is. It has the same succession of limitless horizons, the same dreary monotony. Caravans glide over its surface like gigantic fleets. When a party of Bedouins once came to the Mediterranean, they inquired, "What is this *desert of water?*" There is a wonderful amount of romance about the desert, which explains the charm which it possesses for the sons of Ishmael. The colours of its drifts of sand are glorious in the glow of morning and of evening. Its wonderful mirage presents to view from time to time such regions of delight as may have suggested to the Prophet his vision of the Moslem's Paradise. While ever and anon this tremulous horizon-picture becomes a reality, and we behold the beautiful, mysterious oasis, a place of palms and fountains, a miracle renewed continually and justifying the exclamation of the grateful Arab, "God is great! God is merciful!"

HOUSES OF PARLIAMENT, OTTAWA, CANADA.—In 1858 Queen Victoria selected Ottawa as the seat of the Canadian Government, and it is consequently the capital of the Dominion of Canada. It is a city of only about 40,000 inhabitants, but its Government Buildings would do honour to any capital. They form three sides of a quadrangle and are situated on an eminence 150 feet above the Ottawa river. Covering an area of nearly four acres, their cost was four million dollars. They are substantial and yet extremely ornamental in appearance. The general style of their architecture is Italian-Gothic. The arches of the doors and windows are of red sandstone, and the columns and arches of the legislative chambers are of marble. The roofs are rendered attractive by means of variously coloured slates, and the towers and pinnacles are adorned with iron trellis-work. The interior decorations of this edifice are also very rich and tasteful, including the Viceregal canopy and throne, a marble statue and portrait of Queen Victoria, and full-length likenesses of George III. and Queen Charlotte by Sir Joshua Reynolds. The Library of the Government is a very handsome and valuable portion of this structure, and contains more than 100,000 volumes. Ottawa has in addition to these Houses of Parliament, a fine Cathedral with lofty spires, and an imposing Catholic institution known as the Gray Nunnery. At one extremity of the town are the famous Chaudière Falls, in which the Ottawa river plunges over a rough precipice forty feet high and two hundred feet wide. The "Chaudière" itself (or cauldron) is of unknown depth. The sounding line has not found bottom even with a length of 300 feet. It may perhaps be added that down the Ottawa river, which is the chief tributary of the St. Lawrence, a steamboat makes a daily trip to Montreal (101 miles away) in about ten hours; a pleasant relief from railroad travel.

"THE THOUSAND ISLANDS," ST. LAWRENCE RIVER, CANADA.—Usually a name like that of "The Thousand Islands" is more poetical than truthful, and we smilingly agree to pardon the poetic license of exaggeration. But in this portion of the St. Lawrence river the number of islands actually is nearer 1,500 than 1,000. Their nearness, beauty and variety amaze the traveller. Commencing with Wolf Island, about 30 miles in length, they gradually increase in number, although diminishing in size, forming innumerable combinations, floating apparently at times in groups or else as individuals, and cutting thus the surface of the stream into a maze of intricate channels, which to a tourist appear bewildering. It is a charming day that the traveller spends in sailing in and out along these liquid labyrinths. Some of the "thousand isles" are uninhabited, others are owned by private individuals and hold embosomed in delightful foliage expensive and picturesque villas, whose inmates spend here weeks and months in summer. The names bestowed upon these fair retreats indicate the opinions entertained of them by their enthusiastic occupants. Thus the three islands visible in this illustration are respectively called "Nobby," "Castle Rest" and "Welcome." Hotels are also found at frequent points. Boating and fishing are the principal amusements of the "Islanders," and these are always close at hand.

BOSTON COMMON, BOSTON, MASS.—To a Bostonian the "Common" is almost sacred ground. No matter how crowded are the surrounding streets; no matter how inconvenient it may be to go around it; the Common must remain inviolate. It dates from 1634, and by the city's charter, is made public property forever. It is unusual for a city to have thus in its very heart a park of 48 acres, laid out in sloping lawns and lovely walks; and this is the more remarkable since, divided from the Common only by a single street, is another park of 22 acres called the Public Garden. These two enclosures, adorned with ponds, statuary and beds of flowers, form thus an enormous hollow square of 70 acres, of easy access to thousands. The great beauty of the Common lies in its magnificent elms which make the stately avenues beneath them completely shaded. No reader of Oliver Wendell Holmes can forget his allusions to the Common in his "Autocrat" and "Professor at the Breakfast Table." Above the Common, and shown to the right in picture, rises the handsome State House, with its gilded dome, crowning the summit of Beacon Hill. On one side of it extends a part of Beacon Street, long famous for its fine residences, among which was once the house of John Hancock. Another side is flanked by Tremont Street, now being rapidly transformed into attractive shops. Within a stone's throw of the Common are many prominent buildings, such as the Public Library, the Masonic Temple, Music Hall, the Somerset Club, the Athenæum Library and the State House, already mentioned, as well as the Old Burying-Ground, where repose the patriots, John Hancock and Samuel Adams.

NATIVES OF QUEENSLAND, AUSTRALIA.—Queensland is the latest of England's Australian colonies, having been separated from New South Wales in 1859. Formerly it was a penal settlement, a dumping-ground for incorrigible ruffians, who nevertheless were of great value in cultivating the land and erecting the public buildings of the capital of Queensland, Brisbane. This illustration shows us some of the Australian natives living in the interior, but who occasionally come down to the coast for trading purposes. As has been said elsewhere, in describing Sydney, these Aborigines are a wretched race. Like most savages, they are fond of liquor, and were it not for strict laws prohibiting the sale to them of intoxicating drinks, they would doubtless soon become exterminated through their own excesses. Originally these natives, like the Maoris of New Zealand, were probably cannibals. The latter were in the habit of eating human flesh as late as 1814, when the missionaries first visited New Zealand. Many of these natives tattoo themselves, the number and style of this decoration indicating their rank. The sad fact impresses itself upon the traveller as he looks upon these millions of Aborigines in the South Pacific, that little can be done to improve them. They are doomed. If left alone, and to the gradual development of centuries, they might perhaps evolve themselves into a higher order of humanity. But like the North American Indians, they are disappearing rapidly before a new and sturdier race, and the islands and continents of the great southern ocean will soon be peopled only by their conquerors.

THE RIVER JORDAN, PALESTINE.—The Jordan is to Christians what the Ganges is to Hindoos, a sacred river, hallowed by many religious associations, and visited every year by troops of pilgrims. In a straight line the actual length of the Jordan would be 136 miles, but its many curves greatly increase that distance. It has an ending unlike that of any other noted river on our globe. Most rivers cast themselves at last upon the ocean, which seems a fitting termination for their adventurous careers. But this historic stream of Palestine loses itself at last ingloriously in that briny lake of desolation known as the Dead Sea. Yet it is in the vicinity of that strange body of water that the Jordan is held especially sacred. There is supposed to be the place where the Israelites crossed the river into the Promised Land. There Christ is believed to have been baptized by John the Baptist. As early as the fourth century pilgrims had begun to resort thither in great numbers, as they do to-day and have done ever since. Members of the Greek Church especially attach great importance to baptism in the Jordan, and immediately after the Easter celebrations in Jerusalem, an immense caravan is formed for the expedition. The priests wade into the water, and for hours baptize the crowds of men, women and children, who have come for this purpose from distant lands. Many pilgrims fill bottles and jars with water from the Jordan to take home with them. Occasionally through imprudence the swift current of the river sweeps away a pilgrim, whose mode of death is nevertheless envied by his comrades.

THE PYRAMIDS AND SPHINX, EGYPT.—No photographic view does justice to the Egyptian Pyramids.   Nothing else of human workmanship is quite so impressive as these stupendous **masses** of stone.   The height of the great pyramid, Cheops, shown in illustration, is 482 feet, or twelve feet higher than the cross which sparkles on the dome of St. Peter's at Rome.   If **therefore,** that pyramid were hollow, instead of being almost entirely solid, the whole cathedral of St. Peter's (dome, cross and all) could be contained within it, like an ornament in a glass **case.**   It covered originally thirteen acres, though it has been reduced to eleven acres by the spoliation which went on here for centuries.   Each of its four sides measured at the base 765 feet. **Think** of eighty-five million cubic feet of solid masonry piled here together in one pyramid alone with such accuracy that astronomical calculations have been based on its angles and **shadows!**   Vastly inferior in size to the pyramids but surpassing them in antiquity is the Sphinx, a monster cut out of a natural cliff on the edge of a descent, and partially buried in shining **drifts of sand.**   Horribly mutilated though it be, this relic of Egyptian antiquity stands solemn and silent in the presence of the awful desert, symbol of eternity.   If those mighty lips could **speak,** they might utter the words, ''before Abraham was, I am!''   There it disputes with Time the empire of the past; forever gazing on and on into a future which will still be distant, **when** we, like all the millions who preceded us and gazed upon its face, have lived our little lives and disappeared.

GIBRALTAR.—The ancients believed this cliff to have been planted by the gods at the western limit of the civilized world, beyond which even the boldest never dared to sail. No single illustration of it can reveal its many characteristics. It rises on one side almost perpendicularly from the waves to the height of 1,300 feet. It is three miles long and about half a mile wide. From some positions it resembles a gigantic lion crouching by the sea and guarding thus the entrance to the Mediterranean. Just opposite this on the African coast is a mountain very similar in situation and appearance to Gibraltar. In climbing over this extraordinary fortress the traveller sees a great number of half-natural, half-artificial caverns or galleries, designed to serve as places of protection during a bombardment. Some vegetation covers this apparently barren rock, and frequently the mouth of a cannon grimly protrudes from a bed of flowers. Gibraltar is probably impregnable. It has for many years been in the possession of the English, and has resisted every effort made to capture it or silence its tremendous batteries. The fortress is continually provisioned, and so perfect are the arrangements for a water supply, that at a few hours' notice it can be put into a condition to withstand a year's siege. Although this cliff is almost paved with British cannon and surmounted by the English flag, it is still an eloquent memorial of the Moors. The name "Gibraltar" is a corruption of Arabic words meaning "The Mountain of Tarek," leader of the Moors when they landed in Spain. For more than 700 years it was held by them, till on the fall of Granada, in 1492, they were expelled to Africa.

HALL OF SATURN, PITTI PALACE, FLORENCE, ITALY.—The Pitti Palace at Florence is still used as the residence of the King and Queen when they visit Florence, but it possesses for mankind an infinitely greater value than that arising from its being an abode of royalty. It is a marvellous treasure-house of art, containing probably a greater number of fine paintings than any other building in the world. If Europe should lose every other gallery of art save this, it would still be rich. To copy some of its rare works an artist must make application five years in advance, so many are there who desire the privilege. Moreover, the decorations of the halls containing these pictures are worthy receptacles for the works themselves. The lofty ceilings themselves are covered with paintings framed in gilded and statue-laden cornices. Beneath are exquisitely inlaid floors. Put out your hand, and it may touch a table of mosaic, malachite, or lapis-lazuli, the cost of which was probably £20,000. Sit down to rest, and you perceive that you are in a chair of satin, silk brocade or velvet. Look round you in bewilderment, and you behold elaborately decorated walls, on which from gorgeous roof to sculptured marble dado hang the world's great masterpieces! While even the doors through which we pass have frames of variegated marble. One really needs to make one visit here before he can appreciate a single picture. Close by the door leading into another of these gorgeous apartments one sees in this illustration that sweetest and most tender of all Raphael's paintings, the "Madonna of the Chair."

THE APPIAN WAY, ROME.—Southward from the Eternal City stretches across the Roman Campagna one of the most interesting thoroughfares in the world. It is the Appian Way. The Romans were marvellous road-builders, and this great military highway to the South was admirably constructed two hundred and twelve years before Christ. It is a most impressive hour that one spends in driving on this Appian Way. This desolate Campagna was once so thickly covered with suburbs and villages that it was difficult to tell where Rome ended and its environs began. But now beneath this almost uninhabited plain there seems to sleep a vanished world. On either side for miles we see the vestiges of ruined tombs, for this Via Appia was the fashionable burial place of ancient Rome. The Romans were not fond of quiet cemeteries. They preferred that their bodies should be laid away near some great artery of human activity, where their funeral monuments might still recall them to their passing friends. Some of these tombs were very large; some were undoubtedly extremely elegant. The historic souvenirs of this ancient highway make of the Appian Way one of the most suggestive portions of Italy. Along this road, for example, and between many of these very tombs which we behold to-day came the magnificent funeral procession of the Emperor Augustus, bringing his lifeless body back to Rome for burial. By this route also was conveyed to Rome the beautiful captive, Zenobia, Queen of Palmyra; and from this Appian Way St. Paul first saw the Eternal City as he came to preach there a religion which was to supersede the faith which then prevailed, and ultimately make of Rome the central city of Christianity.

MT. BLANC, SWITZERLAND.—No visit to Switzerland is complete without a trip to Chamounix, that little village above which rises the sovereign of the entire Alps, the first of all upon whose brow at sunrise rests a crown of gold, viz. Mt. Blanc. It is called thus the "*white mountain*," par excellence, from the glittering mantle of eternal snow in which it stands enveloped to the height of 15,781 feet. It is this peak more than any other of the Alps which has enchanted us from childhood, and even before our eyes have rested upon it, we have sung: "Mt. Blanc is the monarch of mountains, They crowned him long ago, On a throne of rocks, in a robe of clouds, With a diadem of snow!" Ever since 1786, when the guide Balmat (after incredible difficulty) gained the summit, thousands have been ambitious of following in his footsteps. Yet in the years which have elapsed since its conquest, only about 1,200 foreigners have reached its crest. And these have been the fortunate ones; while those who failed, or have been frozen, injured or killed outright have far exceeded them in number. Yet, notwithstanding a long catalogue of disasters, we need not be apprehensive here. For the science of the ascent has now been reduced to a system; and with fair weather, good guides, and suitable precautions there is no very serious danger. Moreover, the guides of Chamounix are far too much alive to the profits of their business to bring discredit on either the mountain or themselves by incurring undue risks.

THE RHINE AND COLOGNE, GERMANY.—Of all the cities on the Rhine, Cologne is the wealthiest and most renowned. It has played quite a role even in Roman history. Here Trajan received the summons to assume the Imperial purple. Here Vitellius and Silvanus were proclaimed Emperors; and here the latter was murdered by his cohorts. Here also, in the camp of Germanicus, was born Agrippina, the mother of Nero; and she, retaining an affection for her birthplace, sent here in after years a colony of Roman veterans, and gave it her name, *Colonia Agrippina*, whence comes the modern name *Cologne*. A multitude of churches greets the eye as one surveys this city from the Rhine, but of course its crowning feature is its glorious cathedral in the foreground. Those who beheld that building fifteen years ago would hardly recognize it now. Massive indeed it was and vast, but looking somewhat like the hull of an enormous ship without its masts, since its great towers lacked completion. But now it has a glory and a majesty which lift it heavenward above all other churches in the world. It is unquestionably the most magnificent Gothic edifice upon the surface of our globe. Begun in 1248, it was not completed till 1883. The last stone was placed in its position, amid impressive ceremonies, in the presence of old Emperor William and nearly all the Princes of Germany. Its towers reach an altitude of 511 feet! The nave is 145 feet high from floor to roof! It is impossible to gaze on certain parts of either the exterior or interior of this stupendous structure without feeling well-nigh crushed by an overpowering realization of the sublime.

STREET SCENE IN COPENHAGEN, DENMARK.—Certain localities, like certain people, please us at first sight. We cannot always tell exactly why. The fact, however, still remains. They give us pleasure. That we know. This Danish capital is such a place. It is not handsome architecturally. Most of its streets are narrow and old-fashioned, and yet one likes old Copenhagen well, just as one frequently prefers a plain but kindly face to that of a distinguished beauty. Copenhagen has two very noticeable characteristics, cleanliness and cheerfulness. Its streets would put to shame the usual American thoroughfares. In them one sees not only no dirt, but almost no drunkenness, nor traces of excessive poverty. As for cheerfulness, one rarely finds more general good humour in a populace than here. Of course the Danes have little hilarious gaiety, like that which characterizes the Neapolitans. They seem by contrast *serenely* happy. Their faces beam with calm contentment. Cheerfulness seems with them a universal trait, politeness an invariable rule. Our old friend Hamlet, therefore, as the "melancholy Dane," must have been a national exception. Copenhagen is the birthplace of the great sculptor, Thorwaldsen; and one of the prominent buildings in the city is the Museum reared to contain originals or copies of all his works. In the courtyard of that Museum, surrounded by the masterpieces of his genius, Thorwaldsen lies buried.

NAERODAL PASS, NORWAY.—The "Naerodal" is a magnificent mountain-gorge extending inland and upward from the equally sublime "Naerofjord." It is characteristic of the wonderful coast of Norway, that long arms of the sea, called "Fjords," wind inland from the Atlantic for nearly one hundred miles, bordered by gigantic, gloomy, almost perpendicular cliffs, which approach each other at times so closely that the spray from their countless cascades may be blown over the deck of the steamer as it glides along at their base. At the extremity of almost every such fjord the grooved formation of the coast still continues towards the interior, and no doubt such wild ravines as the Naerodal once contained water; the gradual elevation of the shore having caused the ocean to retire. Ages ago, therefore, human beings, if any had then existed here, could have sailed through this Naerodal, where travellers now drive or walk. Is is a place of great sublimity. On either hand tower dark and almost perpendicular mountains, without a scrap of vegetation on their barren sides, though down their savage, wrinkled faces stream numberless waterfalls. One of these mountains, called the Jordalsnut, has the form of an enormous thimble, and, as its composition is silvery feldspar, it presents a most brilliant and beautiful appearance, especially at sunset or under the refulgence of the moon.

BURNS' COTTAGE, SCOTLAND.—Ayrshire, the "Land of Burns," is one of the most interesting features not merely of Scotland, but of Europe, to those who love to visit places hallowed by the genius of illustrious men. The little town of Ayr abounds in memorials of the poet, one of which is this humble cottage in which Robert Burns was born in 1759. The little bedstead in which he slept was once bought for a mere trifle by a stable-boy, who afterwards sold it for twenty pounds. Everything in the vicinity reminds us of his poems. Not far away, for example, is "Auld Alloway's witch-haunted Kirk," the scene of Tam O'Shanter's ludicrous adventure on that night when Burns tells us "Even a child might understand the De'il had business on his hand." Near here also are the "Banks and Braes of Bonnie Doon," that lovely stream of which the poet has so sweetly sung. It was while pacing up and down the banks of this river one winter's afternoon in 1790 that Burns composed his poem of Tam O'Shanter; and one may see now the very bridge o'er which the terrified Tam rode from the witches for dear life on his gray mare Maggie! It was also while standing beside this stream that Burns and his "Highland Mary" held a little Bible between them (still preserved in the Burns Museum at Ayr), and pledged to each other eternal faithfulness. Between the faded leaves of that Bible now rests a little tress of her hair, and who can forget the sad lines of her lover, as after death he wrote that poem commencing "Ye banks and braes of Bonnie Doon, How can ye bloom sae fresh and fair? How can ye chant, ye little birds, And I sae weary, fu' o' care?" The name of Burns is a household word in Scotland, and he is immortally enshrined in the affections of his countrymen. More than 30,000 strangers visit this birthplace of Burns every year!

MUCKROSS ABBEY, LAKES OF KILLARNEY, IRELAND.—The Lakes of Killarney are exquisitely beautiful features of Ireland, about 50 miles north of Cork and 180 miles south of Dublin. Each summer sees a multitude of American travellers visit them as one of their first experiences in the European tour which they begin by landing at Queenstown. After an ocean voyage almost any cultivated land appears attractive. How much more, then, a conspicuously lovely region like that of southern Ireland! Nor are the Killarney lakes merely beautiful. They have the charm which the Old World imparts to almost every portion of its natural scenery, namely, that of historic association. They are studded with finely wooded islands on which are the ruins of castles, convents and abbeys, around which cluster souvenirs of many centuries. On one island, for example, is Ross Castle, an old fortress of the O'Donoghues; another has the picturesque ruins of the "Sweet Innisfallen" of Tom Moore; while not far from this is Muckross Abbey, built by the Franciscans in 1440. Other abbeys there are in Scotland and England and on the Continent more beautiful than this, but by an American, who has just landed here and to whom this is the first ruin he has seen, it will never be forgotten. The subtle sense of antiquity, which is lacking in his own country, steals insensibly over him, and the accumulated influences of years of reading and anticipation at once assert themselves, and thrill him with the joyful realization that this is but a foretaste of all that now awaits him, outlined before him in a long and beautiful perspective. Yet no matter how much more he may enjoy, the memory of the sentiments awakened in the ivy-mantled walls of Muckross Abbey will abide with him forever as an inspiration.

LONDON BRIDGE, LONDON.—Of all the bridges which cross the Thames within the city limits none is so famous as this which characteristically bears the name of "London." It was opened to traffic by King William IV. in 1831. It is of granite, and its cost was about £1,600,000. The lamp-posts on its sides are said to have been cast from cannon captured from the French during the Spanish war. It had till lately the distinction of being the last bridge on the Thames or the one nearest to the sea, which is about sixty miles away. The restless tide of human life ebbing and flowing across this granite thoroughfare is a suggestive sight. Dickens was fond of studying here by day and night those widely differing phases of humanity, which can be seen in this world-metropolis better than anywhere else on earth. This bridge is never deserted, and during twenty-four hours it is estimated that 20,000 vehicles and 120,000 pedestrians cross here from one side of London to the other. The roadways are so arranged that those who desire to drive rapidly follow one course, and those whose wishes or whose horses are more moderate must take the other. Standing on this connecting link between the two great sections of the World's Metropolis, one realizes the immensity of London. Nearly *five millions* of people live within its mighty circuit. Twenty-five hundred are born and about two thousand die here every week. One hundred million gallons of water are used here every **day,** in spite of the multitude of the "Great unwashed." If the people of London were placed in single file, eighteen inches apart, they would extend 1,200 miles, or further than from Boston to Chicago. There are in London more Roman Catholics than in Rome, more Scotchmen than in Edinburgh, more Irishmen than in Dublin. The poverty and wretchedness in certain quarters of the city are as extreme in one direction as the magnificent display and wealth of the West End are in the other. Yet no great city in the world is better paved or better governed.

PLACE DE LA CONCORDE, PARIS.—This is the most magnificent public square in the world. On one side the Rue Royale extends to the majestic Church of La Madeleine. Opposite to that is the river Seine. On the right of the square, as we here behold it, is the Garden of the Tuilleries, and on the left the famous promenade of the Champs Elysees. In the centre rises the Egyptian Obelisk erected there during the reign of Louis Philippe. It is 76 feet high, and was brought hither from Luxor, a suburb of "ancient, hundred-gated Thebes," where it had been standing more than 3,000 years. On two sides of this historic monolith are imposing fountains, and around the Square we discern eight colossal seated statues representing the principal cities of France: Lille, Bordeaux, Nantes, Rouen, Brest, Marseilles, Lyons and Strasbourg. Since the Franco-Prussian war the statue of Strasbourg has been constantly draped in mourning or surrounded by wreaths of flowers, a touching proof of the affection still felt by the French for that city taken from them by the Germans. The history of this Place de la Concorde is as sombre as the square itself is gay. It was the favourite place of execution during the Reign of Terror in 1793-4. Upon the spot which that Egyptian Obelisk now darkens with its shadow stood then the fatal guillotine which beheaded the King Louis XVI., the Queen Marie Antoinette, the Girondists, Charlotte Corday, Madame Roland, and at last Danton, Robespierre, and the original leaders of the Revolution. Chateaubriand well said, in view of the thousands who had perished there, that "All the water in the world would not suffice to wash away the blood which had there been shed."

BOSTON COMMON, BOSTON, MASS.—To a Bostonian the "Common" is almost sacred ground. No matter how crowded are the surrounding streets; no matter how inconvenient it may be to go around it; the Common must remain inviolate. It dates from 1634, and by the city's charter, is made public property forever. It is unusual for a city to have thus in its very heart a park of 48 acres, laid out in sloping lawns and lovely walks; and this is the more remarkable since, divided from the Common only by a single street, is another park of 22 acres called the Public Garden. These two enclosures, adorned with ponds, statuary and beds of flowers, form thus an enormous hollow square of 70 acres, of easy access to thousands. The great beauty of the Common lies in its magnificent elms which make the stately avenues beneath them completely shaded. No reader of Oliver Wendell Holmes can forget his allusions to the Common in his "Autocrat" and "Professor at the Breakfast Table." Above the Common, and shown to the right in picture, rises the handsome State House, with its gilded dome, crowning the summit of Beacon Hill. On one side of it extends a part of Beacon Street, long famous for its fine residences, among which was once the house of John Hancock. Another side is flanked by Tremont Street, now being rapidly transformed into attractive shops. Within a stone's throw of the Common are many prominent buildings, such as the Public Library, the Masonic Temple, Music Hall, the Somerset Club, the Athenæum Library and the State House, already mentioned, as well as the Old Burying-Ground, where repose the patriots, John Hancock and Samuel Adams.

"THE THOUSAND ISLANDS," ST. LAWRENCE RIVER, CANADA.—Usually a name like that of "The Thousand Islands" is more poetical than truthful, and we smilingly agree to pardon the poetic license of exaggeration. But in this portion of the St. Lawrence river the number of islands actually is nearer 1,500 than 1,000. Their nearness, beauty and variety amaze the traveller. Commencing with Wolf Island, about 30 miles in length, they gradually increase in number, although diminishing in size, forming innumerable combinations, floating apparently at times in groups or else as individuals, and cutting thus the surface of the stream into a maze of intricate channels, which to a tourist appear bewildering. It is a charming day that the traveller spends in sailing in and out along these liquid labyrinths. Some of the "thousand isles" are uninhabited, others are owned by private individuals and hold embosomed in delightful foliage expensive and picturesque villas, whose inmates spend here weeks and months in summer. The names bestowed upon these fair retreats indicate the opinions entertained of them by their enthusiastic occupants. Thus the three islands visible in this illustration are respectively called "Nobby," "Castle Rest" and "Welcome." Hotels are also found at frequent points. Boating and fishing are the principal amusements of the "Islanders," and these are always close at hand.

STRAW COTTAGES, SALAMANCA, MEXICO.—The average dwelling of the poor Mexican Indian is a wretched one. Miserable hovels constructed out of cakes of sun-dried clay, or huts made of all sorts of refuse, such as discarded railroad ties, sugar-cane stalks, old barrel staves and bits of matting—such are too frequently the abode of thousands upon thousands of the natives of Mexico. A blanket, usually of a brilliant colour, is the *real* home of the average Mexican Indian. In that he lives, moves and has his being. Wrapping it to his chin about his thin shirt and trousers of white cotton, he leans against a wall for hours, looking like a soiled barber's pole. When night comes he will change his position to a horizontal one, but his coloured blanket will still envelop him. These Indians are said to be generally happy and contented, but it is hard to believe it in view of their condition. Many of them certainly have a hopeless and even timid look, like that of a well-meaning dog that had been beaten and abused. The old Spaniards found the Aztecs in many respects a cultivated and intelligent race. They slaughtered them, however, by thousands and seized upon their land, like robbers. The Indians have, therefore, had little chance to ameliorate their situation. There are about *seven millions* of them who must be educated and elevated before Mexico can start unfettered on the plane of other nations. This is now being attempted by a system of public instruction, which has in the last few years accomplished good results. As a proof of the capacity of the natives under favourable conditions, it should be remembered that General D. Porfirio Diaz is probably the ablest man that Mexico has ever produced.

ON INDIAN RIVER, FLORIDA.—One of the greatest charms of Florida is the opportunity it affords of sailing through tropical scenery. Several of its rivers are navigable for small steamers, and a more picturesque and delightful experience can hardly be imagined than that of gliding hour after hour between majestic cypress trees, magnolias, palmettos and palms, as through the palm-girt, cypress-bordered avenues of some southern Venice, whose palaces had sunk beneath the waves. It is true there is something gruesome and uncanny in these everglades of Florida. Strange birds fly back and forth above our heads; black snakes are lurking in the shadows of the trees, and alligators float motionless upon the tranquil surface of the stream. To sail through scenes like this *at night*, when the strong headlight of the boat brings out this weird and desolate foliage in startling relief, is something never to be forgotten. The Indian river, represented in this illustration, has a length of nearly 150 miles. The lands adjoining it are very fertile, producing all the southern fruits, from oranges to cocoanuts, in great profusion. This river is especially famous, however, for the almost incredible number and variety of fish which there abound, including the celebrated pompano, mullet and tarpon. Turtles also are found there weighing 500 pounds. Twenty years ago this region was somewhat difficult of access. At present a branch railroad has brought it within easy reach of Jacksonville. The once sparsely settled country is rapidly becoming populated, and on the banks of this stream are several prosperous towns.

WASHINGTON'S HOME, MT. VERNON, VIRGINIA.—A delightful excursion to be made from the City of Washington is the steamboat journey of fifteen miles down the Potomac to Mount Vernon, the home and the burial-place of Washington. The "Father of his Country" came into the possession of this estate in 1752. The wings of the mansion were built by him. Its situation is beautiful, and the view of the river from the house is charming. Thanks to the "Ladies' Mount Vernon Association," as well as to the efforts of the brilliant orator, Edward Everett, this home of Washington together with six acres of adjacent territory is now the property of the nation, having been purchased in 1856 from the President's descendants for the sum of $200,000. The house, which is of wood, contains some objects of great interest, including pieces of furniture used by Washington, also his firearms, portraits and some articles of clothing. Upon the wall hangs the key of that stronghold of tyranny in France, the Bastille, a relic of the French Revolution presented to Washington by his friend and companion-in-arms, La Fayette. Not far from his former home is the tomb of Washington. It is an unpretending structure of brick, approached by an iron gate, through the bars of which one sees the marble sarcophagi containing the remains of George Washington and his wife Martha. The time will doubtless come when the old residence will crumble to decay beyond the possibility of restoration. Then, if not before, let us hope that the Nation will erect a suitable monument to mark the burial-place of its illustrious Leader and Founder, and to remind all coming generations that this lovely hill-side of Virginia is consecrated ground.

UP THE HUDSON FROM WEST POINT, NEW YORK.—Fifty-one miles north of New York City stands the great Military Academy of the United States, West Point. If it had been demanded by its founders that an exquisitely beautiful and peaceful location should be secured for this, nothing more perfect could have been obtained than the remarkable promontory on which this training school for warriors has been placed. The scenery on every side is charming. Glorious indeed are the glimpses which one gains here of the Hudson's winding shores, to which history, poetry and legend give undying interest. Blue in the sun, flecked with light shadows from the passing clouds, or dark and wrathful 'neath a storm, this river is a constant source of pleasure and fascination. Paths of ideal beauty wind about these hillsides, sun-sheltered by the trees and rendered cool and fragrant by the breezes from the moving stream. Old Rhenish castles, it is true, do not remind us here of feudal times, but history has left some traces even on these banks which stir the heart of an American patriot. During the war of the Revolution West Point was one of our most important military posts, from which our troops were sent out to their various battlefields. These hills are also haunted with souvenirs of *Treason.* For who can here forget the infamous attempt of Benedict Arnold to deliver this stronghold to the enemy? The American Nation is yet young, and none can say what great events may not in the future be enacted on the borders of this stream. God grant, however, that its limpid surface may never again be darkened by the shadow of a traitor, until the waves, which peacefully sweep by these wooded hills to-day, shall have commingled with the ocean, shall have been resolved to mist to fall again in showers on the Adirondack Mountains, and once more, possibly ages hence, shall roll in splendour to the open sea.

RUE DE RIVOLI, PARIS.—Few of the many beautiful thoroughfares in Paris are more interesting or better known to the traveller than the Rue de Rivoli. On one side for a long distance it is bordered by the Garden of the Tuilleries, the former site of the Tuilleries itself (destroyed by the Communists in 1871), and the magnificent Museum of the Louvre. A little further, on the same side, rises the handsome Gothic monument called the Tour St. Jacques. The northern portion of the Rue de Rivoli is scarcely less interesting. There are the famous Palais Royal and the Theatre Français, as well as the great Magasin du Louvre, and such well-known hotels as the Continental, the Meurice and the Windsor. The great peculiarity of this street is the line of arcades extending for a long distance on its northern side. These are formed by a projection of the second story of each building over the sidewalk, thus furnishing a promenade completely sheltered from the sun and rain. Here are innumerable shops of jewelry, photographs and fancy articles, and foreigners are continually gathering around the attractive windows, like moths about a brilliant flame. In these arcades one often hears more English spoken than French. This street has been the scene of many thrilling episodes in history. Some of its arches have beheld the tumbrils rolling on to the red-posted Guillotine during the Reign of Terror. Robespierre himself, like the hundreds who had preceded him, was led along this thoroughfare to the gory knife. It also saw the humiliating return of Louis XVI. and Marie Antoinette after their attempted escape; and besides having witnessed many of the dazzling receptions given to Napoleon, its name commemorates one of his most brilliant victories over the Austrians in Italy, the famous battle of *Rivoli*.

SHAKESPEARE'S HOUSE, STRATFORD-ON-AVON, ENGLAND.—The little town of Stratford-on-Avon is famous only as the birthplace of the immortal Shakespeare. Fortunately the house in which the poet was born on the 23d of April, 1564, is now national property and is most carefully protected. Hither come every year about 14,000 visitors, most of them Americans. The building has undergone some changes since Shakespeare's time, but the old timbered framework is the same. On the first floor a little room facing the street is pointed out as the one in which the Bard of Stratford first saw the light. The walls are literally covered with inscriptions, written or carved in every tongue, and indicating thus an endless throng of pilgrims of all ranks, from prince to peasant. Elsewhere these names would be an outrage; but here, in memory of this universal genius, they seem a proof of the spontaneous, world-wide homage of mankind. Among them are the names of Byron, Sir Walter Scott, Thackeray, Dickens, Tom Moore, Washington Irving and the Duke of Wellington. In other rooms are exhibited many interesting relics of Shakespeare, including his portraits, his school desk, several early editions of his works, and his signet-ring. Not far from this house is the lovely church in which all that was mortal of this sublime genius was laid away to rest beneath that weird and well-known epitaph: "Good Friend, for Jesus' sake forbear—To dig the dust enclosed here. Blest be the man who spares these stones, And curst be he who moves my bones!"

FINGAL'S CAVE, SCOTLAND.—Off the western coast of Scotland, and easily reached now by excursion steamers, Nature has placed one of her greatest marvels, namely, the island of Staffa, rising in barren grandeur from the ocean and looking like an enormous table supported by innumerable columns, which rest upon a floor of lapis-lazuli. It is only about a mile in circumference, yet its perpendicular cliffs present a grand appearance, reaching at certain points an elevation of 140 feet, and honey-combed with wave-worn caverns lined with innumerable fluted columns, which in some instances curve outward, as though to more successfully oppose their breasts to the tremendous surges of the sea. The largest of these openings is Fingal's Cave. It is an awe-inspiring place to visit, though when the sea is rough it is impossible to enter it. Its curving roof is nearly 100 feet above the waves, and in calm weather travellers may go in boats far into the heart of the cliff along that pillared vestibule 230 feet in length. At the extreme end of this magnificent cavern is a kind of natural throne, imposing enough to suggest the kingly seat of Neptune himself, and from this the view outward through this avenue of columns, whose pavement is the sea, is beautiful beyond description. When a storm is raging on this coast the scene at Fingal's Cave is said to be sublime. The force of the stupendous billows hurled against these cliffs is then appalling, and the incessant roar emerging from this mighty cavern can be heard for miles. This is indeed a solemn Minster of the sea, wrought ages since by Nature's architect, and Ocean's anthems have resounded here in majesty long before Egypt reared her pyramids or ever human eyes beheld its grand proportions and listened to its awful symphonies.

ROYAL PALACE, STOCKHOLM, SWEDEN.—On one of the islands of the charming capital of Sweden stands an enormous building, conspicuous from almost every part of the city. It is the Royal Palace. Its vast proportions make it certainly imposing, but beautiful it cannot be called, especially on close approach; for its huge walls are covered with stucco, for which the keen frosts of a northern winter have evidently no respect. The interior of the building, although not elegantly furnished, is very attractive from the home-like air of comfort and simplicity which there prevails. One room of special interest is the Council Chamber, a handsome hall adorned with fine oak carvings and old Gobelin tapestries. There every Friday morning King Oscar II. holds a conference with his ministers, and whatever may be the abilities of those who then assemble there, it is safe to say that the King himself is their superior. Oscar II. is no ordinary man. His court, though unpretending, is one of the most refined in Europe. No other sovereign equals him in respect to scholarly attainments, unless it be Pope Leo XIII. He speaks all the prominent European languages, and can at any time address the students of the Universities in an impromptu speech of purest Latin. He long ago acquired for himself a place in Swedish literature, not as a King, but as a private individual, and he is known as a poet, as writer of military works, a contributor to reviews, and a translator from Spanish and German writers. The Swedes have reason to be proud of their King.

MAUSOLEUM OF CHARLOTTENBURG, BERLIN, GERMANY.—The park adjoining the Palace of Charlottenburg, a few miles from Berlin, contains a beautiful marble Mausoleum, the interior of which is represented in this illustration.   It is the burial place of the Prussian King, Frederick William III., and his wife, the idolized "Queen Louisa."   The tombs of Royalty are numerous in Europe, but few can be compared with this for beauty and solemnity.   The walls and floors are all of polished marble, upon which falls a delicately-coloured light from stained glass windows in the roof, while in the centre upon marble couches are these recumbent figures of the King and Queen.   There is a beautiful repose about these statues.   With their folded hands, they seem to lie, not in death, but "like one who wraps the drapery of his couch about him and lies down to pleasant dreams."   Hither, as to a hallowed shrine, each year upon the anniversary of the Queen's decease, the members of the Royal Family come to lay some floral tribute on her grave.   And there are few events in the life of the old Emperor William more touching than the visits which he made to this, his mother's tomb, before and after the late war with France ; the first as it were, to invoke her blessing on the coming conflict ; the last (when flushed with victory) to lay his laurels at her feet !

THE MER DE GLACE, SWITZERLAND.—One of the most renowned of all the Alpine glaciers is the Mer de Glace.   At a distance the vastness of this "Sea of Ice" is but partially disclosed.   Still we can see upon its sides miles upon miles of pulverized rocks ground off from the adjacent cliffs.   Among them, too, are boulders twenty or thirty feet square, now tossed about like nut-shells, the rocky debris of ages.   Between these tracts of earth and stone is an area comparatively white and pure, and (as its name, the "Sea of Ice," would indicate) this looks as if the billows of the sea had suddenly been turned to ice, the crested waves having been instantaneously frozen while in their wildest act of tossing.   At times these waves assume gigantic shape.   For as the glacier pushes downward towards the valley, the various obstructions which it meets distort it into monstrous forms.   Some of these glittering waves are larger than any cathedral man has ever reared, and among them it is quite impossible to move without the aid of ropes and ladders.   There is here a strange contrast between the forces of Life and Death.   This frozen mass steals down between the pastures, tossing its glacial waves close to the trees and hayfields of the meadow, and one may swing a scythe and gather flowers, while perchance only a hundred yards away his neighbour by a careless step may be perishing in a deep crevasse.

EXTERIOR OF THE COLOSSEUM, ROME.—Anticipate what you will, this edifice will not disappoint you. All things considered, nothing in Rome can equal it in grandeur. Its walls are more than 200 feet in height. It is said to have been built by 60,000 captive Jews after the conquest of Jerusalem by Titus. Close by it is a ruined fountain at which the gladiators washed after the combat, surrounded no doubt by a gaping crowd, and petted and admired by effeminate patricians, who with their soft white hands patted the brawny muscles of the athletes and offered wagers on their next success. The corridors of the Colosseum reveal to us huge blocks of stone, placed there apparently by the hands of giants, yet fastened with no cement. There was no danger here of panic, fire or collapse. In fact, woe to the man who trifled with the public in those days! One architect, Attitius by name, did try it once, and made a flimsily constructed wooden edifice, which fell, occasioning great loss of life. Tacitus tells of the catastrophe, and then relates the builder's punishment in three short words, which ought to be inscribed above the door of every wretchedly built theatre in the world; they are these: "Attitius was burned!" For more than 400 years this was the scene of sanguinary gladiatorial combats, and frequently of Christian martyrdom. The arena of this amphitheatre has therefore long been looked on by the Christian church as consecrated ground.

PANORAMA OF FLORENCE, ITALY.—To one who visits the Old World with a keen appreciation of its History, Biography and Art, perhaps no European city proves more attractive than that which greets us here, in beauty, where—"On the bright enchanting plain, Fair *Florence* 'neath the sunshine lies, And towering high o'er roof and fane, Her Duomo soars into the skies!" What a priceless debt of gratitude we owe to this fair Tuscan Athens! A debt so vast that we are quite unable to express its magnitude. After the appalling gloom of the Dark Ages, which, on the downfall of Imperial Rome, folded entire Europe in its shroud, the first pale streaks of light, announcing the approaching dawn of a new age, appeared above these walls of Florence! 'Tis true, the glory which succeeded that bright dawn did not last long. Its splendour scarce outlived two centuries. But in that time Italian art and literature reached their zenith, and Florence ever since has been a treasure-house for those who prize inspiring memories and forms which live again on canvas or in marble. What wonder, then, that this fair city of the Renaissance, girt by its amphitheatre of vine-clad hills, cleft by the current of the smiling Arno, and guarded by the Tuscan Apennines, is not alone a beacon-light in the world's history, but one of the most enchanting spots upon the surface of our globe!

SALON OF MARIA DE PADILLA, ALCAZAR, SEVILLE, SPAIN.—The Alcazar (a name derived from Al Kasr, the house of Cæsar) is a Moorish palace, begun when Arabian Caliphs ruled in Spain in 1181. It was, however, largely rebuilt by the Christian sovereign, Pedro the Cruel, and most of its gorgeous apartments are haunted by the memory of his tragic deeds, which seem to have no fitness for so fair a place. The room portrayed in this illustration is the boudoir of Maria de Padilla, the beautiful lady whom Pedro loved and secretly married. He was, however, subsequently forced into a political marriage with the French Princess, Blanche de Bourbon. Three days after, he left the wife he hated for the woman he loved, and the unhappy Blanche was cruelly persecuted, imprisoned several years, and finally put to death. Maria de Padilla seems to have been unable to restrain Pedro from committing revolting crimes within this very palace, one of the worst of which was the murder of his illegitimate brother, whom he caused to be struck down by the maces of his courtiers, and whose blood-stains are still pointed out in one of these marble pavements. Six years later Pedro himself was stabbed to the heart. The Alcazar of Seville is in some respects more beautiful than the Alhambra. At all events its Moorish ornamentation has suffered less from the ravages of Time and Man. Its exquisite tile-work and the stucco tapestry of its walls are like mantles of finely-woven lace. Behind this palace are lovely gardens, laid out by Charles V., and abounding in myrtle hedges and orange groves, bright with their glistening leaves and fruit of gold. The windows of this apartment command a view of these gardens, and no doubt the beautiful Maria de Padilla has often looked out upon their charming terraces and breathed their perfume-laden air, perhaps as a slight consolation for having ever married Pedro the Cruel!

PALACE AND HAREM, ALEXANDRIA, EGYPT.—A German poet has said that Alexandria resembles an orphan child who has inherited from his father nothing but his name. In fact, almost nothing of its ancient glory is now visible. Even its obelisks, popularly known as Cleopatra's Needles, have within the last few years been carried thence to London and New York. Some wealthy residents from the various parts of the world still make Alexandria their home, and occasionally we see there the abode of a Pasha, whose high walls and lattice windows hint of the beauty which may there be concealed. Few cities in the world, however, have occupied so conspicuous a place in history as ancient Alexandria. Founded and named after himself by Alexander the Great, 332 B. C., it became the greatest centre of commerce on the Mediterranean, the principal seat of Grecian learning, the place where St. Mark first proclaimed the Gospel, and finally a prominent stronghold of Christianity. It is also the half-way house to India, the door-way of Egypt, and the gate of the Red Sea. The Alexandrian School was one of the most remarkable that has ever existed. Among its scholars were Strabo, the geographer; Hipparchus and Ptolemy, the astronomers; Archimedes, the mechanician, and Euclid, the mathematician. Its famous library, when it was burned in Cæsar's time, numbered about 900,000 volumes! Here it was that the Old Testament was translated from Hebrew into Greek; and this once beautiful city has beheld the revelries of Antony and Cleopatra, and the murder of Hypatia. It now has a population of about 200,000, of whom 50,000 are Europeans. But its glory has departed, and though it is still interesting as a cosmopolitan city and a commercial metropolis, the traveller feels that it is now only an introduction to glories beyond, and is eager to advance inland to the ruins of old Egypt, and to "Cairo, the Magnificent."

VALE OF CASHMERE, INDIA.—So much has been written of the beauties of the Vale of Cashmere that it has become almost an ideal locality—a sort of Utopia. Mohammedan writers have descanted extravagantly on its beauties, and the poet Moore, taking these as a guide and with modern additions, has built up a great part of his romantic descriptions of this lovely vale. And yet, when we consider the beautiful aspect of this valley in its different phases—its fresh green foliage of Spring, its many-hued autumnal tints, together with its glistening snow-capped mountains, and the quiet glassy river meandering through its shadowy groves, we think few will say that romance has drawn a too vividly coloured picture of its loveliness. The **Vale of Cashmere** (or Kashmir) is an enclosed and elevated valley in the Himalaya mountains, north of the Punjab, through which flows the river Jhelum. It is about 120 miles in length and its greatest width is about 75 miles. The valley has, in modern times, been a resort for English sportsmen, but quite recently the shooting has been carried to such an extent that game is only found in the most secluded ravines and on the more difficult hill-sides. Among the game found here has been antelope, ibex, musk deer, wild goat, brown and black bear and leopard. The convolutions of this river winding through miles upon miles of cultivated fields, which resemble in the distance Oriental rugs, undoubtedly suggested the general designs of the beautiful Indian shawls produced here with such labour and highly prized throughout the world.

HARBOUR OF AUCKLAND, NEW ZEALAND.—Auckland has been called the Naples of New Zealand, and the Corinth of the South Pacific, because of the beauty of its situation by the sea. It is the first port touched at by steamers going from Honolulu to Sydney, Australia. Its climate is so salubrious that it is regarded as a health-resort. To the average American New Zealand is almost unknown, and he hardly realizes that here on the other side of the globe is a flourishing city of 70,000 inhabitants, with hospitals, public libraries, museums, theatres, opera houses and botanical gardens, while a submarine cable keeps it "in touch" with all the rest of the world. The whole of New Zealand is subject to earthquakes, which nevertheless do not seem to interfere with its prosperous development. In one small area it is possible to count sixty volcanic cones! On that account until recently this city was almost entirely built of wood. In the suburbs of Auckland are extensive forests of great value. Their large straight trees, often one hundred feet in height, are said to make the best ship-timber in the world. These trees are valuable also, not merely from their wood, but from a peculiar gum which they produce, and which is exported in large quantities. This gum is a deposit, not of the living tree, but of the dead ones! It is found usually several feet below the surface of the tree, which sometimes has a diameter of fifteen feet. It looks like amber, and is principally used in the manufacture of varnish. New Zealand consists of three islands, the area of which is almost equal to that of England, Scotland and Ireland. From its extensive seaboard, therefore, it closely resembles the mother country.

HAVANA, CUBA.—Cuba is naturally a wonderfully fertile and productive island, blessed with a charming climate and delightful scenery. But, as in many other portions of the world, man has too frequently undone and spoiled all that indulgent Nature has so lavished here. Insurrections, revolutions and conflicts with Spanish soldiery have ruined many miles of territory once covered with large estates of sugar, coffee and tobacco. What the city of Havana might become commercially under more favourable conditions can be easily imagined, when we consider its own beautiful situation and the marvellously rich country behind it, of which it is the natural gateway. Excellent steamers now bring the traveller from New York in four days to this lovely bay on which Havana is located. So popular has this trip become that good hotels have been constructed here, which in the winter months are often crowded with foreigners. The view across the harbour from some of the upper rooms of these hotels is of great beauty. Of course Havana is essentially Spanish in architecture, customs, language and amusements. Bullfights are as much the delight of the Habaneros as of the inhabitants of Madrid and Seville; and famous Matadors come over here from Spain to win new laurels in Cuba, as European Opera Singers cross the Atlantic to New York. As is well known, in Cuba are produced the finest specimens of the tobacco plant which the world knows, and a genuine "Havana" is almost an object of devotion to every lover of the "fragrant weed."

MUIR GLACIER, ALASKA.—There is probably no natural feature in the world more awe-inspiring and sublime than the stupendous Muir Glacier in Glacier Bay, Alaska. In the rear of it are mountains 15,000 and 16,000 feet high. Into the bay itself advances with a glittering front 300 feet high and *over a mile in length* a frozen river, moving steadily and resistlessly at the rate of forty-four feet a day during the summer months! Further inland it has a width of three miles, and is fed by fifteen minor glaciers! Excursion steamers approach it as closely as safety permits, and there, filled with emotions too profound for words, one gazes on this slowly-moving, solidified Niagara, from which huge icebergs fall at frequent intervals with explosions resembling the discharges of a cannon. The noise of these falling monsters is well-nigh incessant, and interspersed with these reports one hears weird sounds within the glacier itself, caused by the terrible grinding and compression of millions of tons of ice between the mighty cliffs through which this frozen torrent moves out towards the sea. In front of it is always a large fleet of icebergs, born that day from the parent-mass and sailing out in splendour 'neath a brilliant sun or else in sullen majesty beneath the clouds, to float thenceforth upon the ocean, till they lose themselves forever in its warm embrace. Moreover, this glacier extends not only 300 feet in *height above* the waves, but 400 feet *below* them! Think of the awful power represented here, forever pushing outward from this mountainous interior this gigantic wedge! No words can paint the glories of this wall of ice when it is illumined by the radiance of the setting sun. It then appears the birthplace of innumerable rainbows or a mountain of prisms. The name of this great marvel of the world was bestowed upon it in honour of Professor Muir, the State Geologist of California.

THE CAPITOL, WASHINGTON, D. C.—Every American has reason to be proud now of the central city of his Government. Its miles of asphalt pavement, its broad and extensive avenues, its imposing public buildings and its many elegant residences render it a very beautiful and attractive city. Particularly impressive is the Capitol itself. Its noble dome, 300 feet in height, is a conspicuous object from all portions of the metropolis, and verifies the poet's line, "A thing of beauty is a joy forever." One never wearies of beholding it, so fine are its proportions and so elegant are its graceful curves, making it look like a great marble bell, surmounted by a bronze statue of Liberty. A beautiful park surrounds the hill on which the Capitol is located. One enters it through lofty iron gates and makes the ascent through flower beds, terraces and fountains, to reach at last a broad plateau, upon which stands this grand assembling-place of the representatives of our great Republic. The corner stone of the central part of this majestic edifice was laid by Washington in 1792. On either side of this is a white marble wing, 142 feet long and 239 feet deep. These spacious structures to the right and left of the magnificent dome give an idea of grandeur and solidity well worthy of the Nation which they are designed to serve. The view from the balconies of the Capitol is extremely fine and extensive, embracing the entire city, the windings of the Potomac, the soldiers' cemetery at Arlington, and the hills of Virginia. On the lawn in front is Greenough's colossal statue of Washington, upon the pedestal of which are the well-known and truthful words: "First in war, first in peace, and first in the hearts of his countrymen."

NEW YORK AND THE BROOKLYN BRIDGE.—"On se fait a tout avec le temps," ("One gets accustomed to everything in time,") is a true proverb. No doubt the old Egyptians hardly glanced at their gigantic Pyramids after a dozen years of familiarity with their stupendous forms. So now the people of New York and Brooklyn find nothing specially extraordinary in this great belt of steel and iron which unites their cities, simply because they have at last become accustomed to beholding it. It is, however, one of the marvels of the world. Each of its mighty towers rests upon a caisson constructed of yellow pine timber, which on the Brooklyn side is forty-five feet, and on the New York side seventy-eight feet below the surface of the water. The towers erected on these enormous foundations are one hundred and forty feet in height and fifty feet in width at the water line. The bridge itself is suspended from four cables of steel wire, each about sixteen inches in diameter, and having a deflection of one hundred and twenty-eight feet. The central span across the East river from tower to tower is 1,595 feet long. The entire length of the structure is 5,989 feet. It is eighty-five feet wide, and contains a central promenade for foot passengers, two railroad tracks, along which trains of cable cars are run every three minutes, and two roadways for carriages. The height of the floor of the bridge in the centre to high-water mark is one hundred and thirty-five feet, so that navigation is not impeded. The construction of this noble specimen of engineering skill was begun in January, 1870, and was completed in May, 1883. Its cost was about fifteen millions of dollars. The fare across by car is two cents, and foot passengers are free. About 150,000 people cross it daily.

HOTEL DE VILLE, PARIS.—This magnificent structure has been built to replace the old Hotel de Ville, burned by the Communists in 1871. Its exterior is imposing not only from its grand proportions, but also from the splendour of its decorations. Domes, towers, windows and even chimneys are all adorned with statuary or elaborate carvings. Upon the walls there is a veritable population of illustrious Parisians, and on the roof are ten colossal gilded figures representing heralds, summoning, as it were, the people of Paris to this, their City Hall. The courts and council-chambers of this edifice are also lavishly decorated with paintings and statues. One cannot look upon this modern structure without recalling the old Hotel de Ville which was its predecessor. It played a most important part in the great Revolution of 1789. Thither the destroyers of the Bastille were led in triumph. There the ill-fated Louis XVI. assumed the tricoloured cockade before the maddened populace. Within its walls, after his arrest, Robespierre attempted suicide; and from its steps in 1848 Louis Blanc proclaimed the establishment of the French Republic. It seems incredible that Frenchmen could have been found capable of destroying that historic structure. But on the 20th of May, 1871, the Communists placed barrels of gunpowder and petroleum in its noble halls, and, when compelled by the Government troops to vacate the building, they set fire to the combustibles prepared for destruction. Many of the miscreants, however, perished in the conflagration which ensued, or were shot down by the infuriated soldiery. Thus it is in Paris. Behind her stateliest palaces and athwart her brightest streets and squares falls the grim shadow of some tragic episode in history. Yet, after all, these startling contrasts give to Paris that charm of human struggle and adventure, which no brand new and unhistoric city ever can possess. The difference is akin to that between a young recruit arrayed in bright new uniform and weapons never used save on parade, and some old warrior of a hundred battles, whose body bears the scars of conflict and on whose blunted sword are stains of blood.

THAMES EMBANKMENT AND OBELISK, LONDON.—One of the greatest recent improvements in the World's Metropolis is its embankment along the Thames. The wall next the river is of granite and is backed with solid masonry eight feet thick and forty feet high. This makes a handsome driveway 100 feet in width, lighted by electricity, planted with trees, and having several landing-piers for the river steamers. One of the most remarkable relics of antiquity which the world possesses stands now upon this river-thoroughfare. It is the Egyptian Obelisk, popularly known as "Cleopatra's Needle," which was, however, hewn from the primitive volcanic granite, 1,500 years before that "Siren of the Nile" ever ensnared by her beauty Cæsar and Marc Antony. To convey this from Alexandria to England, as was done in 1877, proved a very expensive and difficult undertaking. Even after it had been success-fully embarked at Alexandria, the little iron vessel which had been specially prepared for it was shipwrecked and temporarily abandoned in the Bay of Biscay. A passing steamer rescued it and towed it into the harbour of Ferrol on the Spanish coast. Thence it was conveyed to the Thames, and finally was erected here where it now stands in triumph. Yet one can hardly look upon this symbol of the sun's bright rays, here in this city of fogs and smoke, without regarding this ancient monolith as an exile from a land where through the entire year the sky is rarely darkened by a cloud. Nevertheless, like many illustrious exiles, its sojourn on the Thames embankment will no doubt be of use to those who gaze upon its stately form, by reminding them of the power and glory of Ancient Egypt, beside whose awful ruins London seems the creation of yesterday.

THE TROSSACHS, SCOTLAND.—The romantic lake-region of Scotland is one of the most attractive parts of Europe, not only from its natural beauty, but because of the charm which Sir Walter Scott's poems and "Waverley" novels have given there to mountains, lochs, rivers and castles. The scenery is not Alpine in his grandeur, nor like that of Norway in sublimity; but it is exceedingly picturesque and beautiful, while its variety of rugged mountains, limpid lakes, soft sylvan scenery and wooded islands renders a tour through this country one of rare delight. Moreover, the region is of limited extent. If pressed for time, the tourist may go from Glasgow to Edinburgh and see the most conspicuous features of the Trossachs in a single day. If the weather be fine, the pictures which unfold themselves at every turn in this poetic and historic country will hang forever in the gallery of the traveller's memory; for everywhere he there beholds, "Crags, knolls and mounds confusedly hurled, The fragments of an earlier world," and "Mountains that like giants stand, To sentinel enchanted land!" Yet frequently to offset this grandeur, we see a tranquil stream or ivied bridge, a peaceful valley or a ruined castle, which give to this delightful scenery an added charm. Moreover, the greater part of this district of the Scottish lakes (so sparsely is it populated) seems like a pleasure-park reserved for tourists. For the old Highland Chiefs have long since disappeared, and the few wealthy land-owners spend often only three or four weeks here on their vast estates to entertain their guests, or shoot the game upon their hills.

THE ROYAL MUSEUM, BERLIN.—A very prominent structure in Berlin and another glory of the Unter den Linden is the Royal Museum. Its situation is superb, fronting upon a handsome park adorned with trees and flowers. Its very dimensions are imposing. A noble portico of Ionic columns gives it an air of strength and majesty, while its great height is proved by the four groups of statuary on the roof, which, though colossal in themselves, appear on such a pedestal diminutive. At the foot of the broad staircase, leading to the Museum, is an enormous basin of polished granite, sixty-six feet in circumference and weighing seventy-five tons, yet hewn out of a single granite boulder, left ages ago as a memento of antiquity by some huge pre-historic glacier within thirty miles of the future Berlin. The Art treasures in the Berlin Museum are not so numerous nor so valuable as those in some other European galleries, for Berlin is young, and when the great Frederick began to collect masterpieces of the past there were comparatively few that could be obtained. Nevertheless, the selections have been so carefully made that no lover of art can afford to miss the Museum of Berlin. This Royal Museum was founded by Frederick William III. in 1824. To this has been added a "New Museum," especially rich in Egyptian relics, and casts of ancient, mediæval and modern sculpture. Its most attractive feature, however, to the traveller is probably the series of magnificent frescoes, designed by Kaulbach, on the staircase of the New Museum. Though modern works, Michael Angelo would doubtless have admired them. They illustrate the history and development of the human race, from such great events as the overthrow of the Tower of Babel, the heroic Age of Homer and the destruction of Jerusalem, to the exploits of the Crusaders and the Age of the Reformation. These frescoes alone are enough to give to Berlin a unique position in the realm of the fine arts.

INTERIOR OF THE COLOSSEUM, ROME.—This is indeed the King of Ruins. Around it are eighty mighty arches leading to its interior. The 87,000 people who were often seated here could find abundant means of entrance and of exit. One might suppose that all the pictures he had seen of the interior of the Colosseum would leave no room for astonishment. But neither word nor photograph quite prepares one for the grand reality. These rows of ruined arches, rising in a gigantic circle toward the sky, are overpowering in their immensity. The countless doorways seem like caverns in a mountain side, from which wild beasts might even now emerge. Those who beheld this twenty years ago would hardly recognize the interior of the Colosseum as it now appears. Around the sides were formerly little chapels dedicated to the memory of Christian Martyrs who had here found death. Here every Friday afternoon a sermon would be preached, teaching how much the Christian faith once cost, yet how that faith has lived and triumphed over Cæsarian Rome. But now the greater part of the arena has been opened to the light. One sees the subterranean cages for the animals, the corridors through which they rushed to the arena, and the apartments where the gladiators waited till called to duty, probably to death. Gigantic as it is, almost as much of the Colosseum seems to have disappeared as still remains. In the fourteenth century it was looked upon as a legitimate quarry from which to extract building material. Four thousand workmen were at one time employed in tearing down its walls, and some of the largest palaces of Rome were thus constructed.

COURT OF ORANGES AND MOSQUE, CORDOVA, SPAIN.—The Mosque of Cordova is one of the most splendid relics of the Moors which can be found in Spain. The very approach to it is beautiful. One steps in through a Moorish gate and finds himself at first in this fine old courtyard, containing cedars, cypresses, orange-trees three centuries old, and palm-trees of unknown antiquity. A perfect wave of perfume greets one as he enters it, like that which meets him when he enters a conservatory. In the centre is an ancient fountain, at which birds stop to drink, women to fill their pitchers, and "Children of the Sun" to lie within its shadow and live apparently on the juice of an orange and the throbbing tones of a guitar! The Mosque itself has been transformed into a Christian church, but nothing can conceal the special character given it by the Moors, namely, that of *a marble forest*. For there one still sees more than 1,000 monolithic columns of marble, jasper, porphyry or pure alabaster, forming a truly bewildering multitude of glittering paths of softened light and shade! An edifice like this recalls the glory of Cordova in the days of Abdurrahman the Great. Then (about 1,000 years ago) there were within the walls of this city six hundred mosques, fifty hospitals, nine hundred public baths, six hundred inns, eight hundred schools, and a library of 600,000 manuscript volumes; and hundreds of students went here daily to the Moslem schools, where Music, Medicine Philosophy and Mathematics were then taught, as nowhere else in the world.

MODERN ATHENS, GREECE.—The rank which nations have acquired in history is not dependent on their size. Greece was the smallest of all European countries. Yet in the light of the stupendous influence exerted by a few Athenians in the days of Phidias, China's four hundred millions seem like shadows cast by moving clouds. The debt which the world owes to Greece in general and to Athens in particular is beyond computation. Her language, her literature, her temples, her statues, together with her philosophers, orators, historians, statesmen and heroes, kindle the soul to-day with the inspiration of true genius, immortally associated with such names as Socrates, Plato, Pericles, Aristotle, Herodotus, Demosthenes, Phidias and Xenophon. If most of her art-treasures had not been carried away from Greece, first to embellish Rome, and finally to fill the various museums of the world, Athens would be now annually visited by thousands instead of hundreds. Nevertheless, its Acropolis is still here, together with many of its ruined shrines and numerous sites of classic and historic interest. The modern and the ancient parts of the city are in close proximity, and therefore one enjoys modern luxuries and comforts in full view of some grand memorials of the past. The palace of the present able sovereign, George I. (son of the King of Denmark) stands only a few hundred yards from the Acropolis, and from the windows of our hotel we may look off on the classic mountains of Hymettus, Pentelicus (where were the quarries of Pentelic marble), and Lycabettus, the one displayed in the illustration. A charming blending this of old and new! For though the streets are modern, their names upon the corners are traced in the same characters which Socrates pronounced and Plato wrote.

AVENUE OF SPHINXES, KARNAK, EGYPT.—Karnak is the most stupendous temple ever reared by man, and is to-day one of the most amazing ruins which the sun beholds in all its course. Even this approach to it must have been overwhelming in its grandeur. It was an avenue nearly two miles long, and sixty-three feet wide, bordered by hundreds of colossal Sphinxes, the fragments of which still remain. Nor was this the only such approach to Karnak. Ten others, almost as imposing, have been traced! Four thousand years ago this avenue and the temple to which it led were in their glory. The archæologist, Champollion, has truly said: "The imagination sinks abashed at the foot of Karnak." Such a temple as this is in its way almost as marvellous and awe-inspiring as the Pyramids themselves. It transcends all our previous ideas of what had been either probable or possible. The ruins of Karnak seem to-day more like those of a city than a temple, thrown into terrible confusion by a succession of earthquake shocks. It thrills one to survey this chaos of upright or overturned columns, walls, gates and obelisks, and to realize that as long ago as the time of Joseph, magnificent processions of Kings, priests and worshippers made their way between these very Sphinxes, now headless and disfigured, awed by the grandeur of this unrivalled Vestibule.

CAPERNAUM, GALILEE, PALESTINE.—The Sea of Galilee is still as blue and beautiful beneath the Syrian sun as when the Saviour walked beside its shores or sailed upon its surface. But its surroundings are now desolate. The city of Tiberias is a most wretched, unattractive town, and proud Capernaum is such a ruin that doubts are entertained as to its site! There is no trace here now of any quay or harbour; but in the midst of a great mass of ruins rise the remains of a fine old building made of white limestone resembling marble. It must have once been an imposing edifice, for scattered there in great confusion are many ruined columns and elaborate capitals. This, it is thought, must have been the Synagogue of Capernaum. If so, within its walls the voice of Jesus was frequently heard. The Gospels tell us of his visit to this place, and of his prophecy of its humiliation, which certainly is startlingly verified to-day. How little did the people of Capernaum imagine, as they disdained the utterances of the Nazarene and his humble followers, that the time would come when even the situation of their city would be a matter of dispute, and if an object of interest at all, that it would be so, merely because that gentle Teacher who addressed them had once walked its streets! Beyond the ruined town is the fair lake, sixteen miles long and six miles wide, bordered by undulating hills, whose rounded forms are just the same as when the gaze of Jesus rested on them, and when He uttered on their graceful slopes words which have revolutionized the world.

NATIVE VILLAGE NEAR CALCUTTA, INDIA.—How many people in America realize that India is 1,600 miles wide, and has 240,000,000 inhabitants, who speak thirty different languages, which vary as much as the different tongues of Europe? Life for most of these natives is reduced to its lowest terms. Three yards of cotton cloth furnish their dress, a little rice their food, and fifty cents a week their probable income on which to support a family! It would seem as if Nature invented means to cut down this enormous population. Occasionally famines sweep away thousands at a time. Cholera and other pestilences claim their victims too at frequent intervals. In one year 18,000 deaths from snake-bites have been recorded in India. One tiger in India was known to have killed 110 persons before it was shot! But human life increases rather than decreases there, notwithstanding these appalling scourges. These natives are not black like Africans, nor red like the American Indians. They are pure Asiatics, of a dark brown colour. Those who have even rude dwellings are better off than thousands of their fellows; for in many places men, women and children may be seen sleeping in the streets and on the country roads, wherever their fatigue has induced them to find rest. Alas! the pitiably degraded condition of the great majority of the population of India is disheartening, and almost incredible to one who has not investigated the subject. There is no doubt of the ancient grandeur and civilization of India, and of the vast debt we owe her for her noble Sanscrit language (the parent of so many others), and for many precious truths in science and religion; and this it is which makes us feel a greater sadness as we see the painful proofs of her decay.

YOKOHAMA, JAPAN.—Yokohama has not the best of conveniences for landing visitors. There are, in fact, no suitable piers. Shallow water obliges vessels to anchor half a mile off shore, and passengers are landed from the steamers in tug boats. The harbour itself, however, is good, and one beholds there steamers and ships from all parts of the world, including many powerful war vessels belonging to Russia, England, the United States or Japan. Innumerable little fishing boats and small trading ships are also moving about, for the Japanese are skilful sailors, and spend much time upon the sea which penetrates their numerous islands at so many points. Beyond the city, although seventy miles away, rises the silvery cone of the great Japanese volcano, Fujiyama. Forty years ago Yokohama was a small fishing hamlet, but to-day its population is nearly 140,000. Its streets are finely macadamized and remarkably clean, and its general appearance is that of a bright and active commercial town. To the foreigner, however, it is merely a doorway (somewhat European in character) leading to the real Japan beyond. Thus only eighteen miles away, and less than an hour's ride by rail, is Tokio, the Japanese capital, containing nearly a million of inhabitants, and covering an area about as large as that of London.

MT. CHIMBORAZO, ECUADOR, SOUTH AMERICA.—This most famous of all the mountain peaks of the Andes, 21,400 feet in height, was for many years supposed to be, not only the highest summit of the Andes, but the highest in the world. But after years of adventurous travel and more accurate measurements, it is now found to rank only as the sixth in height. The Nevado de Sorata, now acknowledged to be the loftiest mountain peak of this famous group, reaches the altitude of 25,300 feet, or nearly four thousand feet higher than its more famous rival. Mt. Chimborazo is surrounded by high tablelands, above which it rises only 12,000 feet; so that, stupendous as it is, its enormous altitude can only be fully realized when viewed from a great distance. Humboldt and his party of explorers made most extraordinary efforts in 1802 to reach its snow-crowned pinnacle, but with all their strenuous exertions they only succeeded in reaching a point about 2,000 feet short of its summit. The whole party suffered intensely from the usual inconveniences of such high altitudes, breathing with difficulty and the blood bursting from their eyes and lips. They found themselves surrounded by thick fogs and in an atmosphere of the most intense cold. They made unusual efforts to gain a still higher point, but found themselves entirely blocked by an utterly impassable chasm, and in this vast field of unfathomed and unfathomable snow, were compelled to reluctantly commence the descent. In 1831 an attempt was made by another traveller, Bousingault, to reach the summit, but he also failed, although he succeeded in arriving at a point about 250 feet higher than Humboldt had done, viz. an altitude of 19,689 feet. Its summit was twice reached in 1880 by Mr. Edward Whymper, the famous Alpine traveller. The appearance of this peak from the Pacific coast is peculiarly grand, and although 200 miles distant, it is distinctly defined against the blue sky.

PANORAMA OF THE CITY OF MEXICO.—The view of Mexico from the Cathedral towers is beautiful. You then perceive at once the situation of this Capital of the Montezumas. It lies almost in the centre of a valley encircled by mountains. In the distance, glittering like a belt of quicksilver, is a line of six lakes, which have often been a source of peril to the city on account of disastrous inundations. Immediately below the towers is the Plaza Mayor, the great square of the city, which was 400 years ago an open space in front of the Aztec temple. On one side of this extends the enormous National Palace, built by the Spaniards more than two hundred years ago. Since that time it has been the headquarters of the various governments with which poor Mexico has been blessed or cursed. There lived, for example, during their brief reign, Maximilian and Carlotta, ill-fated victims of Napoleon's dream of empire in this western world ; there President Diaz has his official rooms to-day ; and within its large enclosure are the National Museum and the Post-office. Upon the space which this enormous structure occupies rose formerly the Imperial residence of the Aztec Sovereigns. In looking down thus on the City of Mexico one recollects that at the time when Cortez captured and destroyed it, it was a kind of Venice. The Indians, for purposes of defence, had chosen a lake for their abode, and Mexico was thus intersected by miles of those liquid streets so charmingly described by Prescott in his story of the Conquest. The Spaniards, however, filled up most of the canals, and in process of time the lake itself dried up and disappeared. On a clear day from the Cathedral towers the grand volcanoes, Popocatepetl and Iztaccihuatl, are distinctly visible, rising like cones of frosted silver on the sky.

TOTEM POLES, ALASKA.—In front of the rude cabins of Alaska Indians rise frequently tall, hideous posts sometimes 100 feet in height. They are called Totem Poles. From top to bottom they are usually carved into grotesque resemblances to human faces or else to forms of bears, wolves, birds and fishes. Just what they signify is not always clear. Some certainly commemorate heroic deeds in the lives of those beside whose homes or graves they are erected. Some also indicate by certain marks, resembling coats of arms, the family or tribe to which the dead may have belonged. One totem pole, for example, may represent a bear and a gun, rude symbols doubtless of the fact that the man whose memory is thus evoked once shot a bear, and probably under some peculiar circumstances deemed worthy of commemoration. Most of them are three or four feet in diameter and about thirty feet high ; though some attain an altitude of sixty, eighty and even one hundred feet. The height of the pole is supposed to have denoted the rank of the deceased. Some of the natives value these ancestral relics to such a degree that they refuse to part with them at any price ! It is supposed that only rich natives could have had the honour of a totem pole. The carving, however crude it may seem to us, represented a great deal of time and labour for the native sculptor. Moreover, it was customary to give a grand banquet, free to all comers, whenever such a pole was raised. Hence one of these decorated family ornaments probably involved, in all, an expenditure of several hundred dollars.

THE WHITE HOUSE, WASHINGTON, D. C.—The real name of this building is the *Executive Mansion*, but it is almost universally called the White House. It is a plain but somewhat imposing edifice, built of freestone painted white. It is only two stories high, but the effect of this is relieved by the eight Ionic columns which support the lofty portico of the main entrance. The first Executive who occupied this was President Adams in 1800. Since then it has been the abode of every Chief Magistrate of the Republic. The grounds adjoining and belonging to the White House comprise about seventy-five acres, twenty of which are inclosed as the private garden of the President. The latter are not, however sufficiently walled off to afford the Executive or his family any real privacy within their limits. The principal apartment in the White House is the "East Room," a richly decorated parlour eighty feet long and forty wide. This is usually open to the public daily from 10 A. M. to 3 P. M. The President's Study and the Cabinet Room are on the second floor, as are also the private apartments of the family. The history of the White House is of course the history of the country, so far as the latter has been affected by the distinguished men who have occupied in turn the Presidential chair; and no American can regard without emotion this stately though unostentatious building, beneath whose roof have lived Abraham Lincoln and Ulysses S. Grant.

MAMMOTH HOT SPRINGS, YELLOWSTONE NATIONAL PARK.—This is the northern entrance to that most wonderful section of the United States, which Congress has very properly "dedicated and set apart as a public park or pleasuring grounds for the benefit and enjoyment of the people." Every year the wonders of this National Park are becoming more known to those for whose use and pleasure it has been reserved. It is sixty-five miles long and fifty-five miles wide, and all of it is more than 6,000 feet above the level of the sea. Its mountains have an altitude of from 10,000 to 12,000 feet, and wear continually their mantles of dazzling snow and ice. The geological features of this region are most extraordinary. Within its limits there are no less than fifty geysers which throw up columns of water from 50 to 200 feet in height, and volumes of steam to a much greater altitude! It also contains probably 10,000 hot springs, whose water varies in temperature from 160 to 200 degrees! The famous Yellowstone lake, near the southeast corner of the Park, is one of the most beautiful bodies of water in the world, twenty-two miles long, nearly 8,000 feet above the sea, 300 feet deep, clear as crystal, and surrounded by snow-covered mountains from 3,000 to 5,000 feet higher still. Here, too, are the Falls of the Yellowstone river, 360 feet high; the wonderful calcareous deposits known as the "Grand Terraces;" and, most remarkable of all, the *Grand Canyon*, whose almost vertical walls, only a few hundred yards apart, rise to the height of 1,500 feet. Between these, when one looks *down*, the river seems like a vein of silver in a mountain gorge; and when one from the bottom of the cañon looks *up*, he sees merely a narrow line of sky, like a blue river curbed by granite banks. The varied colours in the stone composing this great chasm produce a combination here unsurpassed in the world.

THE BOURSE (OR EXCHANGE), PARIS.—A handsome structure is this edifice where fortunes are so easily made and lost. Surrounded by sixty-six Corinthian columns, this building is not unlike the model of a Temple in the Roman Forum. When the traveller has seen the Stock Exchange of New York or the Board of Trade in Chicago, there is nothing especially new or strange in the transactions of this Paris Bourse. Nevertheless the tumult and incessant uproar which wake the echoes of these walls from twelve o'clock to three are well worth noting, as an indication of the feverish excitement of the "Bulls and Bears," whose characteristics do not differ materially, whether the arena where their combats take place be in Wall Street or by Lake Michigan, in the vicinity of the Thames or here in Paris. To stand in the gallery of this Bourse and watch the pandemonium below, or merely, as one lingers on these steps, to scrutinize the faces of successful or unfortunate speculators as they leave the building, affords an admirable chance to study interesting phases of human experience. This square, or "Place de la Bourse," is a great point of arrival and departure of the Parisian omnibusses, the demand for which is usually greater than the supply. But no such crowding is possible here as in our public vehicles in America. Each passenger is entitled to a seat, which he secures by applying for a "number," at the office in the square. The rule of "first come, first served," is rigidly enforced, and when the seats in the coach are filled it rolls away, displaying over its door the word "*Complet*" (full). Who does not recollect the story of the disappointed tourist who exclaimed that the only place in Paris he did not go to was one called "Complet." "Whenever I see an omnibus going there," he cried, "it will never stop for me!" 6

"OLD FATHER NILE," VATICAN, ROME.—Beneath the arches of the Vatican reclines in Oriental calm this mighty statue of antiquity, portraying the Egyptian river-god. It was discovered about 300 years ago buried in that wondrous soil of old Rome, within which no doubt lurk even now so many other masterpieces of the past. The work is full of truthful and suggestive symbols. The figure leans against a Sphinx just as the river in reality flows calmly on before that monster's steady gaze. One hand maintains a cornucopia, a most appropriate emblem of the fertility caused by the river's annual overflow. Over its huge limbs and shoulders play sixteen pigmies representing the sixteen cubits of the yearly rise of the Nile. One of these figures stands erect in the cornucopia with folded arms, as if he symbolized the last or sixteenth cubit, and stood in the midst of agricultural abundance complacently surveying the result. It is not strange that the ancients deified the Nile, for without the alluvial deposit of its fruitful overflow the whole country would be a desert. Egypt is really the gift of Old Father Nile. Just as far as its beneficent waters advance in their annual uprising, just so far extends fertility. Beyond that line is the pitiless desert, between which and the Nile a ceaseless conflict has waged since history began. Ordinarily the inundations of a stream occasion calamity, but those of the mysterious Nile are hailed with thanksgiving and its advancing waves are looked upon as prophecies of peace and plenty.

HADDON HALL, ENGLAND.—Almost in the centre of England stands this ideal specimen of an old baronial mansion, known as Haddon Hall. In the twelfth century it came into the possession of the Vernon family, who occupied it for 400 years. Then when the beautiful young heroine of this castle, Dorothy Vernon, eloped with the son of the Earl of Rutland, the estate passed into the hands of the Rutlands, who still own it, although it is now uninhabited save by its custodians. It well repays a visit, if only for the revelations it affords of the style and decoration of these ancient princely homes of England. The Drawing Room, for instance, now contains no furniture, yet is a grand memorial of ancient splendour. The entire floor is of solid oak, made from a single tree which grew in the neighbouring park. The walls and ceiling are of the same material, their numerous panels beautifully carved with knightly crests and coats of arms. While the huge fire-place with its antique andirons seems waiting to be filled again with blazing logs. In such a place we half expect to see some of the former occupants of Haddon Hall, arrayed in velvet, silk and jewels, discussing in exciting tones the loss of Armada or the escape of Mary Queen of Scots. One also views with interest here the staircase down which, on her sister's wedding night, fair Mistress Dorothy ran with slippered feet to meet her suitor, and the place where mounting the horses waiting for them the lovers rode away through the summer night and next morning, in Leicestershire, were pronounced man and wife.

THE BOURSE, BRUSSELS.—Everyone knows that Brussels is called a "miniature Paris," but few can realize how remarkable the likeness is until they see it. No actual fac-similes of course exist in edifices or in streets; but in the first place the same language is employed in Paris as in Brussels; the same signs greet us everywhere; the colour of the buildings is the same light hue which makes the French metropolis so charming; while even the shops, cafés and covered galleries in Brussels are quite Parisian in appearance. The elegant structure displayed in this illustration will at least call to mind the Paris Opera House. It is, however, merely the Bourse. But what a magnificent building for a Stock Exchange! Yet it is characteristic of the city. Brussels is wealthy. Belgium is progressive. It can not boast of an extensive territory, but it resolves to make the little which it *does* possess not only prosperous, but beautiful. In fact, on some accounts, is not a small, well-governed European monarchy like this much better off, as the world goes, than one which must maintain an enormous standing army and is continually fearing war? So it would seem at least with Belgium, whose policy appears to be: "Let others shake the tree. I will pick up the fruit." This beautiful Exchange was completed in 1874 at a cost of £400,000. But its expense will surprise no one who examines its elegant sculptures, columns and statues, which are even more conspicuous and imposing within than on its exterior.

THE TOWER OF LONDON.—No building in this greatest city of the world is historically so impressive as old "*London Tower.*" Its gloomy battlements watch grimly o'er the Thames as they have done for centuries. Some of its deep foundations are said to be as old as the time of Julius Cæsar. At present, its most conspicuous feature is the massive structure in the foreground, with four pinnacles called the White Tower, built early in the reign of William the Conqueror, about the year 1079. The White Tower! A strange name truly for any portion of this building! For not only are its walls most dark and gloomy in appearance, but behind them have transpired some of the blackest deeds of English History! How many noble men and women have been imprisoned here whose names not only stand transfigured on the pages of history, but have been carved in tears upon their dungeon walls. Among them brave Sir Walter Raleigh, who languished here for thirteen years, part of the time in a small room but ten feet long and eight feet wide! Here all the distinguished prisoners of the Scottish wars were held in close captivity, and hence the noble Wallace was led forth to brutal death and mutilation! Here also was beheaded the noble and innocent Lady Jane Grey; here Anne Boleyn walked calmly to the block, praying with her last breath for her husband. Every spot within the old walls has its own recollections, most of them tales of gloom and pain. At the present day the old Tower is used partly as an armoury and partly as a museum. It is only here and there, and for a moment or two, that the visitor can conjure up the pictures of the fierce historic past.

HARBOUR OF HAMBURG, GERMANY.—Hamburg is located on the river Elbe at the mouth of one of the tributaries of that stream—the Alster. Its harbour is a very extensive one, but, as it now exists, it is a modern creation. At first this city was at some distance from the main branch of the Elbe, and the mouth of the Alster served as its port, but owing to vast engineering enterprises, the principal current was diverted to its present course. The quays of Hamburg now cover a distance of about three miles, and beside some of them are pleasant promenades planted with trees. Vessels drawing fourteen feet of water come up to the city itself, and their cargoes are distributed by means of barges to the warehouses, which line the numerous canals which intersect the town, and make more than sixty bridges a necessity. This harbour of Hamburg presents, as the illustration before us makes evident, a very animated scene. The river is always covered with a multitude of ships and steamers, some of them close to the shore. There is said to be room here for 400 ocean vessels, and for twice that number of river craft. We can hardly be surprised, therefore, to learn that Hamburg ranks first of all the seats of commerce on the Continent, sending its ships and steamers out to every portion of the world. Hamburg is a very ancient city, having been founded probably by Charlemagne in the year 809. In its vicinity are many pretty villages, beautiful promenades and charming villas.

SISTINE CHAPEL, VATICAN, ROME.—One of the most celebrated and important apartments in the Vatican is the Sistine Chapel, called thus from Pope Sixtus IV., who caused it to be built in 1473. It is a lofty hall about one hundred and fifty feet in length, with a gallery on three sides. The upper part of its walls is ornamented with fresco, painted by famous artists of the fifteenth century, and also with many portraits of the Popes, twenty-eight of which are by the celebrated Botticelli. But that which gives to this chapel its greatest artistic value are the works of Michael Angelo which it contains. These are seen first upon the ceiling, which is covered with his magnificent pictorial representations of Old Testament scenes, such as the creation of Adam and Eve, the expulsion from Paradise, and the Deluge. Here are also portrayed in majestic proportions twelve seated figures of Prophets and Sibyls, which are among the most remarkable creations that Art has ever produced. At the end of the chapel, opposite the entrance, is Michael Angelo's enormous fresco of the Last Judgment. This was designed by the great artist when sixty years old, and was completed by him in 1541, after a labour of nearly eight years. In order to show him his appreciation of the work, the Pope himself went to Michael Angelo's house, accompanied by ten cardinals; which, according to court etiquette, must rank as a greater honour than that offered to Titian by Charles V., when the latter picked up the artist's pencil; although the REAL sovereign in both cases was a man of genius. This Sistine Chapel is used for important Papal ceremonies, especially during Holy Week.

GENEVA, SWITZERLAND.—The most beautiful and most populous of Swiss cities is Geneva. Its situation is delightful. Lying at the southern end of its incomparably coloured lake fifty-five miles in length, it commands also a charming view of the snow-clad chain of Mt. Blanc, and is within a few hours' drive of Chamounix. The old part of the town, though clean, is not especially attractive; but all the new portion of the city bordering the lake is enchanting. Handsome bridges cross from one shore to the other above the arrowy waters of the river Rhone, which here emerges from Lake Geneva with crystalline clearness. In the centre of the stream, and reached by one of these bridges, is the sharply pointed "Island of Rousseau," containing a bronze statue of that famous novelist and philosopher, who has made the region of this lake so well known in his romance of the "Nouvelle Heloise." The quays of Geneva are ornamented with stately hotels and elegant jewelry shops, which make of this part of the town a miniature edition of a Parisian boulevard. The excursions which can be made from Geneva to Vevay, Montreux, the castle of Chillon, Lausanne (the home of Gibbon), and Ferney (the abode of Voltaire), all close beside the lake, render this city a charming place of sojourn. The historic souvenirs of Geneva are also full of interest. Its prominent position at the time of the Reformation is of course well known. Geneva was the home of Calvin himself. In or near it also have lived many illustrious literary geniuses like Gibbon and Madame de Stael, to whom the world is forever indebted.

THE FORUM, ROME.—It is a thrilling moment when one looks upon this square, which constituted once the centre of civilization and the brain of the immense Roman world. This was the point from which the roads led out to the extremest limits of that mighty empire subject to the Cæsars, and in this very area stood the golden milestone from which such distances were measured. It is a difficult thing for one to trace with accuracy now the ancient glories of this Forum. We see at various points arches and columns, pedestals and crumbling walls; but what is left is nothing to what once existed here. Eight stately columns tell us of the Temple of Saturn, erected here 490 years before the birth of Christ. Three others rise as relics of the Temple of Vespasian. The Arch of Septimus Severus also is still well preserved. Upon the polished surfaces of some of these the hands of Scipio or of Cæsar may have rested! Pillars are standing here which may have echoed to the voice of Cicero! The memories of this place are therefore such as render it a spot to visit and revisit, not with a throng of thoughtless tourists, but meditatively, with some congenial friend or else alone. One often smiles to see this Forum passed by with a hasty glance by those who little realize that here the famous Roman laws were framed while savages were hunting on the site of Paris, and Britain was an almost unknown region of Barbarians.

ABBOTSFORD, SCOTLAND.—This home of the great novelist and poet, Sir Walter Scott, is an intensely interesting object to visit. It was his own creation. He even planted many of the noble trees in its adjoining Park. Its very ground was dear to him, for it had formerly belonged to the Abbots of Melrose, and was near Melrose Abbey, whose beauty inspired Scott to write some of his most beautiful stanzas. Yet this was not merely a poet's home. It was a veritable battle-field, where one of the noblest sons of Genius took arms against a sea of troubles, which would have paralyzed a braver heart than his. The failure of the publishing house with which he was connected threatened him with ruin, and to save this dearly loved estate, yet pay to the utmost every creditor, became the one great object of his life. Payment was deemed impossible. But Scott knew no such word, and actually assumed the entire debt of about £120,000, asking only for time. In four years he had realized for his creditors nearly £80,000; working ten, twelve and often fourteen hours out of the twenty-four. Never, before or since, was such a sum thus earned. It was Sir Walter's custom to do a vast amount of literary work early in the morning before his numerous guests had thought of stirring, and when everyone supposed him to be still asleep. It was this habit of early toil which enabled Scott to preserve for so long a time his incognito as the author of the Waverley Novels. Here, on September 21st, 1832, the noble-hearted Scotchman passed away from earth while the members of his family knelt around his bed, and his eldest son kissed and closed his eyes. No sculptor ever modelled a more majestic image of repose.

THE MAHMUDIYAH CANAL, EGYPT.—This great work was constructed by the famous Viceroy of Egypt, Mohammed Ali, in 1819. His intention was to connect thus the city of Alexandria with Cairo and the Delta of the Nile, and at the same time to supply the former city with Nile water. He succeeded, but at a fearful cost of human life. He forced 250,000 of the peasants of Egypt to work here like galley-slaves, and 20,000 of them are said to have perished from exposure and inhuman treatment. The cost of the canal in money was about three hundred thousand pounds. This artificial river is wide and deep enough to be traversed by barges and small steamers, and where it receives its supply of water from a branch of the Nile, its banks are lined with solid brick masonry. There are also four engines, of 100 horse-power each, which give an impetus to the water so as to make it flow towards Alexandria. The construction of this canal has been of immense benefit to Egypt. Wherever the waters of the Nile are carried, there can be found life and fertility. Beyond the reach of its waves lies the region of Death—the Desert. The great occupation of the people, therefore, is now, as it was thousands of years ago, *irrigation*. Only bring the water to the land in the seasons, when the river does not overflow its banks, and the Nile will make it glow with beauty and fertility. What a marvellous river, therefore, is this! Hemmed in on east and west by scorching deserts it nevertheless rescues from their withering grasp the two long strips of territory on either bank, which formed the marvellous Egypt of antiquity, and constitute the Egypt of to-day.

VOLKSGARTEN AND THESEUM, VIENNA.—Closely adjoining the Viennese boulevards and not far even from the Imperial palace, is the celebrated Volksgarten, or People's Park, of the city. Vienna is famous for its popular pleasure resorts, and this is one of the most attractive. Its flower-beds, shady walks and pretty fountains are thoroughly bright and tasteful in appearance, and hence most characteristic of Vienna. There, too, surrounded by a multitude of tables, is the music stand, that invariable feature of all Viennese parks. For in no city in the world can one hear so often and so universally that style of music which stirs the pulse and makes one feel good-natured with the world. Here on summer afternoons and evenings may be seen well-dressed civilians, handsome officers, pretty Viennese ladies, all, apparently, without a shade of care or sadness; the scene is one of Southern merriment and vivacity, and we no longer wonder that the Viennese enthusiastically sing of their loved capital: "Es giebt nur eine Kaiserstadt, Es giebt nur ein Wien!" The little marble structure in this park is called the "Theseum," because until quite recently it contained the noble group in marble by the sculptor Canova, representing the conflict between Theseus and the Centaur. But this has now been removed to the new Imperial Museum.

CONSTANTINOPLE AND THE BOSPHORUS, TURKEY.—If there be one city in the world whose site combines in absolute perfection, beauty and utility, and which, while radiant with loveliness, holds the most enviable location on the globe, it is beyond a doubt *Constantinople*, the favourite of Destiny, enthroned upon the threshold of two continents, and well named the "Sultan's Paradise." How matchless is its situation! Here Europe and Asia advance and gaze into each other's eyes. Between them speeds that ocean current called the Bosphorus, which sweeps along in majesty for fifteen miles, connecting the Black Sea and the Sea of Marmora. It is the most secure and capacious harbour that ever opened its bosom to the navies of the world, and lies here like a bridge of lapis-lazuli uniting thus the Orient and the Occident. The oldest part of Constantinople, called Stamboul, is a gracefully rounded promontory, the extremity of which is known as "Seraglio Point." On one side of this, and at right angles to the Bosphorus, is a glittering arm of the sea bearing the title of the "Golden Horn." Just as the Bosphorus divides two continents, so does the Golden Horn separate Constantinople into two great sections, the Turkish (Stamboul) and the European (Galata and Pera). The general view of this capital of the Sultan is one of the most remarkable and beautiful that the world can offer. For aside from the exquisite contour of its wave-washed shores, one looks upon a marvellous perspective of many-coloured houses, marble mosques and palaces, besides numerous graceful minarets which cut their outlines on the clear, blue sky, like columns of polished ivory.

THE PONTE VECCHIO, FLORENCE, ITALY.—The most picturesque, as well as the most ancient, Florentine bridge which crosses the river Arno is the Ponte Vecchio, or "Old Bridge." Old indeed it is, having been built more than 500 years ago. In the centre of it is a pretty portico with three arches, affording delightful views up and down the stream. For centuries the sides of this bridge have had some shops of jewellers and goldsmiths, clinging to it, like barnacles to the sides of a ship. Above these the line of small windows indicates a passage way, formerly called the Gallery of the Grand Duke. It was built to connect the Palace of the Uffizzi on one side of the Arno with the Pitti Palace on the other. Now that both of these splendid palaces are art museums open to the world, this corridor is freely used by tourists; for as is plainly seen in this illustration, the Ponte Vecchio is continued, after it reaches each bank, by this covered corridor uniting one building with the other. The sight of this old bridge is sufficient to recall more or less vividly all the great events of Florentine history. Almost every famous citizen of Florence, from Michael Angelo to Benvenuto Cellini has often crossed that bridge and leaned upon the parapet of its Loggia. Nor has fiction failed to impart to this fine old structure a veil of romance. In George Eliot's matchless novel, "Romola," it was from the arches of this Ponte Vecchio that Tito, to escape the mob, leaped downward through the darkness into the river, there to swim onward into the open country, where, as he landed in exhaustion, he met the fate that he deserved—*death*, by the feeble hands of the old man he had betrayed.

ADOBE HOUSES, NEW MEXICO.—In "New" Mexico and in "Old" Mexico there is a peculiar style of architecture which is both primitive, natural and economical—it is the *Adobe* method of building. Large flat cakes of sun-dried clay, called "Adobe bricks," are used to-day and have been used for ages in these countries. In fact, we find the same thing to have been done in Egypt and the Holy Land, and many a town in Mexico presents a decidedly Oriental appearance on account of its thousands of flat-roofed houses of adobe. It can not be said of this material that it is at all beautiful. The colour of such houses is far from cheerful, being frequently a sort of compromise between a loaf of brown-bread and a strong cigar. There are rarely any windows in these huts and almost never does a chimney rob them of their flatness and monotony. But as a rule in New Mexico, as in the country south of the Rio Grande, no fires are needed either for warmth or cooking, save such as can be made in a pan, or at best, in small brick ovens, heated with charcoal. One-half the world, it is said, does not know how the other half lives. To see these dwellers in adobe huts is quite a revelation to most travellers; but who knows whether their inhabitants are not in reality as happy as the wealthy inmates of a sumptuous palace?

CLIFF HOUSE AND SEAL ROCKS, GOLDEN GATE, CALIFORNIA.—On the southern side of that beautiful entrance to San Francisco Bay, known as the Golden Gate, stands the Cliff House. As its name indicates, it is located on a cliff rising abruptly from the sea, and the view from its broad, shady piazzas overlooking the apparently boundless ocean is one of which no visitor can ever become weary. At a little distance from the hotel are a few ledges, called the "Seal Rocks," over which scores of sea-lions may be continually observed climbing up their steep sides, plunging into the waves, and roaring with delight in tones which make themselves distinctly heard above the breaking of the surf. These animals are protected here by the law of the State, and hence are perfectly fearless and natural in their movements. Some of them weigh at least 1,000 pounds, and these are evidently the masters of the herd which claim the sunniest places on the rocks, and hold them by the principle that "might makes right." The Cliff House is a favourite place of resort, as can be well imagined. In addition to the attractions already mentioned, its restaurant is famous for its excellent cuisine. Behind it are the lovely gardens of Mr. Adolph Sutro, the millionaire, and into these the public is admitted free of charge. Moreover, the drive of six miles hither from the city is one of great beauty, winding through the Golden Gate Park, which comprises more than 1,000 acres, one-half of which are laid out in walks, lawns, flower-beds and drive-ways. In this charming park is a music-stand, in front of which stands a fine statue of Francis Scott Key, the author of "The Star Spangled Banner."

ARCH OF TRIUMPH, PARIS.—One has to deal with superlatives in Paris. To say that this is the finest triumphal arch in the world is a strong statement, but it is literally true. It was begun by Napoleon I. to commemorate his marvellous victories in 1805 and 1806. Built after the style of the old Roman arches of triumph, it nevertheless surpasses them both in its grand dimensions and in the magnificent effect which it produces. Something of this is due to its unrivalled situation. It stands upon an elevation from which radiate, in perfect symmetry, twelve of the finest avenues in existence. The grandest of these is the world-renowned Champs Elysees. Numerous marble reliefs upon this arch commemorate the achievements of the French. Around the summit are marble medallions in the form of shields bearing the names of various brilliant victories. Within the arch are the names of 656 generals of the Republic and Empire. On each of its four immense pilasters is a colossal group of statuary in relief, of which the ones presented in this illustration portray Napoleon crowned by Victory, and France summoning her children to take up arms in her defence. One can form some idea of the grandeur of this structure when he reflects that it is 160 feet in height and 146 in breadth.

KENILWORTH CASTLE, ENGLAND.—Few ruins in all England are more interesting than those of this grand old baronial castle, originally founded by Geoffrey de Clinton about 1120. Queen Elizabeth finally gave it to her favourite, the Earl of Leicester, and he spent enormous sums of money in enlarging and improving it. Sir Walter Scott's novel, "Kenilworth," gives us an idea of the magnificent style in which Leicester entertained the Queen here in 1575. Unfortunately in the time of Cromwell this, like so many other noble structures in England, suffered much mutilation. The clinging ivy, however, makes portions of these ruined walls more beautiful than they could have been when perfect and entire. The material of this castle is old red sand-stone, and hence when illumined by the sunset light its walls and towers glow like shafts of jasper or porphyry, or the volcanic cliffs on the Island of Capri. It must have once been a most splendid residence, well worthy of the abode of him who even dared to hope for the *hand* of Queen Bess, as well as for her *favour*. Its outer wall enclosed a space of seven acres, and ten thousand soldiers were required to guard it. The historic memories of this place appeal to us more powerfully than those of any other castle in England. Instinctively the words of Tennyson here recur to us:

"The splendour falls on castle walls,
And snowy summits old in story;
The long light shakes across the lakes,
And the wild cataract leaps in glory."

MELROSE ABBEY, SCOTLAND.—The charm of this celebrated structure is proverbial and it well deserves its reputation. Its noble columns, windows and arches are of exquisite beauty and delicate carving, and justify this poetical yet accurate description of Sir Walter: "Thou wouldst have thought some fairy's hand,'Twixt poplars straight, an osier wand, in many a freakish knot had twined; Then framed a spell when the work was done, And changed the willow wreaths to stone." This magnificent Abbey was built by King David I., in the twelfth century, and many of the monarchs of Scotland were buried here. Here is also deposited the heart of Robert Bruce. So durable is the red sandstone in which they are chiselled that the most delicately-sculptured capitals and flowers are still perfect, save where the hand of *man* has injured them. Yes, the "hand of man," for the mere lapse of time would not have caused such overthrow as this. Alas! It has been almost universally the fact that man himself has shattered the most exquisite and wonderful structures which human genius has been able to create. So was it here. Again and again contending armies plundered it, and finally the Scotch Reformers did even more injury to its remaining statues and carving than had been effected by the ravages of war! The sight of this ruined pile at moonlight can never be forgotten and imparts forevermore a new charm to the well-known lines of Scott: "If thou wouldst view fair Melrose aright, Go visit it by the pale moonlight, When buttress and buttress alternately Seemed framed of ebony and ivory; And home returning, soothly swear, Was never scene so sad and fair."

COBLENTZ ON THE RHINE, GERMANY.—One of the most important of Rhenish cities is Coblentz, which lies at the meeting point of the Rhine and the Mosel. The waters of the streams do not at once assimilate. The Mosel preserves for a long time its emerald colour quite distinctly, as though unwilling to mingle its French waters with the waves of Germany. The historic souvenirs of this town are extremely interesting. The Romans founded here, 1,800 years ago, a city known as "Confluentia." Hither, after the death of Charlemagne, came his grandsons to divide between them his gigantic empire. In recent times it was a favourite residence of the Empress Augusta of Germany, wife of old Kaiser William. A bridge of boats connects this city with the opposite bank, where on a lofty hill, 400 feet in height, rises the celebrated fortress of Ehrenbreitstein, appropriately called the "Gibraltar of the Rhine." It is a stone Colossus effectively protecting this most important confluence of the two streams, and capable of instantly transforming the peaceful romance of the river into a tragedy of blood and iron. It is safe to say, therefore, that Coblentz will never pass out of the possession of the Germans; for the "Broad stone of Honour" which thus guards it is held to be impregnable, and day and night in massive majesty maintains its perpetual "Watch on the Rhine."

GALLERY OF BATTLES, VERSAILLES.—One of the most imposing and interesting of all the splendid apartments in the palace of Versailles is what is called the "Gallery of Battles."
It has a length of about four hundred feet, and is lighted from the roof, which is made of iron. It is, as the name denotes, a gallery dedicated to the glorification of the God of War.
Around the walls are eighty marble busts commemorating famous generals of France, and above these are some of the finest paintings of battle-scenes that Art has yet produced.
Naturally they all portray the glories of the armies of France in early and in recent times, from Charlemagne to Napoleon. The Napoleonic paintings are particularly fine and represent in
startling force and vividness such victories as Austerlitz, Jena, Friedland, Rivoli and Wagram. This and the many other picture galleries at Versailles are therefore not mere exhibitions of
art, they are illumined tablets of history, calculated to awaken patriotism and stimulate the youth of France to acquire a knowledge of their country's history and to emulate the heroic deeds
immortalized here upon the glowing canvas. Like all the other National Museums of France, this Palace of Versailles is freely open to the public and can be enjoyed and utilized by the
humblest peasant. It is greatly to the credit of the Germans, when they occupied this palace during the siege of Paris in 1871, that they carefully covered these paintings and preserved them
from injury, although many of them represented humiliating defeats which their fathers suffered under the iron hand of the first Napoleon.

COMEDY THEATRE, SCHILLER PLATZ, BERLIN.—The Germans are the most sensible people in the world in regard to their attendance at the Opera or Theatre. Recognizing **the** educational benefit to be derived from good music and fine dramatic performances, the officers of the Prussian army are obliged to go a certain number of times every month to carefully selected places of amusement. The best theatres are financially assisted by the Government, so that a high standard of dramatic excellence and a reasonable scale of prices can be maintained. As for the citizens themselves, they are so fond of the Opera and Drama that they wish to attend more frequently than they could possibly do if late hours were thus always necessary. Accordingly, even in Berlin, the hour for beginning is often half-past six or seven, so that by ten o'clock the opera is over. Moreover, contrary to the system in England, Italy and France, ladies are allowed in the parquet and (blessed rule!) all hats and bonnets are removed. The result of this is an audience which does not spend much thought on dress, but rather has assembled for the enjoyment of the piece performed. The attention therefore is remarkable and no applause is heard until an act is finished. Some other rules pertaining to dramatic performances here are also excellent. Thus, should you take a cab to the theatre outlined in this view, the driver would halt somewhere near the statue of Schiller, or at all events a little distance from the building, and collect his fare, so that, when in the crowd about the entrance, there shall be **no delay**.

LAKE MAGGIORE, ISOLA BELLA, ITALY.—The Italian lakes, Como and Maggiore, resemble precious stones which differ in form and colour, but are of equal value in the eyes of the lover of Nature. Lake Maggiore, as its name denotes, is the larger body of water, being thirty-seven miles in length and four and one-half in width. Moreover, much of the frame-work of this crystal mirror is grander than the one which forms the setting of Lake Como. One of its most attractive features is the Isola Bella, that far-famed island which we here behold, floating like a medallion on the bosom of the lake. Two hundred years ago this was a barren rock ; but Count Borromeo caused to be transported thither a great mass of earth, and converted it, as if by magic, into a series of beautiful gardens rising on terraces 100 feet above the waves. Now, therefore, it is like a fragment of the Orient which has by chance drifted hither ; for lemon trees, magnolias, laurels, magnificent oleanders and other features of the south now flourish there in profusion. Who can wonder at the praises which have been lavished on Lake Maggiore? For, in addition to this island, the shores themselves present a constant series of darkly purple hills flecked here and there with white-walled castles and convents ; while on the shore in every sheltered nook some picturesque Italian village glitters in the sun, or else innumerable villas line each bank in beautiful succession, gleaming like jewels in the dark setting of the trees.

THE MARINA, CAPRI.—The island of Capri in the Bay of Naples when gilded by the dawn, mantled in purple by the sunset light, or turned to massive silver by the moon, must always be sublimely beautiful! It is a huge volcanic rock, three and one-half miles long, crouching on the water like a monstrous Sphinx, whose head and shoulders rise 2,000 feet above the waves in such colossal magnitude that one might deem it sculptured here in grandeur by the gods themselves! The landing place is surrounded by huge boulders towering above the waves, like mighty piers to which this siren-haunted island has been moored, lest it should float away to gladden other coasts. Thither the Emperor Tiberius came about thirty years after Christ, and has bequeathed to this enchanting island the souvenirs of tragedy and shameless vice. For on this rock, guarded by vessels night and day, he thought himself secure at least from poison and the dagger. He built here twelve imperial palaces which rivalled in their size and splendour some of the proudest buildings of the Eternal City. Now nothing is left of these upon the land save dreary vaults and arches ; but in the sea, below a single one of them, tons upon tons of white and coloured marble have been found, with many fine columns and mosaic pavements. Standing on this island and looking out on the unrivalled beauty there disclosed, one appreciates as never before the lines :

"My soul to-day is far away
  Sailing the blue Vesuvian Bay,
  My spirit lies with watchful eyes

Under the walls of Paradise !
  Here Ischia smiles o'er the liquid miles ;
  And yonder bluest of the Isles,

Calm Capri waits
  Her sapphire gates
  Beguiling to her bright estates ! "

LISBON, PORTUGAL.—Lisbon has well been called the "Sultana of the West," for its situation almost rivals that of Constantinople. For from the broad and glittering Tagus it either rises on a series of high hills, or lies in indolent repose for six miles on the water's edge. If close inspection only confirmed the picture which Lisbon presents at a distance, Don Luis would possess the most magnificent of European capitals. Philip II. made a great mistake in not establishing the capital of his empire at Lisbon. If he had done that, Spain and Portugal would probably be to-day a prosperous and united realm. Lisbon would then be the natural sea-port of the whole Spanish peninsula, for the mighty river Tagus, which has its outlet here, actually extends inland for hundreds of miles into the very heart of Spain, like a great arm to gather up its wealth and bring it to the Atlantic, to be thence carried out to Europe, India, the United States or Brazil. There are some handsome streets and squares in Lisbon, particularly prominent among them being the Place of Commerce, which is surrounded by the Exchange, the Custom House, the Treasury and other public buildings, together with a line of open arcades, where merchants gather in great numbers. On one side this great square looks out upon the river Tagus. The commerce of Lisbon has fallen off greatly since Portugal lost Brazil, the brightest jewel in her crown, but there may come a time, if the Spanish peninsula ever is united and well governed, when its prosperity will again be worthy of its once splendid promise and temporary fulfilment.

RUINS, THEBES, EGYPT.—Four thousand years ago there lay upon a plain, 600 miles inland from the Mediterranean and cut by the Nile into two unequal parts, a city which was to the ancient world what Rome was in the days of Hadrian, the Egyptian capital of Thebes. It so abounded in magnificent palaces, statues and temples, that their very ruins form to-day the marvel of the world and attract travellers from every quarter of the globe. Among its wonderful features, still in a measure preserved, are the two colossi, one of which was the famous "Vocal Memnon" of antiquity; and the overturned statue of Rameses II., which was the largest figure ever made by man, one solid block of beautifully polished stone weighing 900 tons! In Thebes also was the stupendous temple of Karnak, unsurpassed in grandeur, as well as many obelisks of great size and beauty. Homer called this city "Hundred-gated Thebes," but investigation has established the fact that Thebes was not surrounded by a wall. The "gates" referred to, therefore, are supposed to have been the splendid entrances to the many temples of the place, some of which are still standing. There is something indescribably mournful in the sight of the mutilated fragments of this once magnificent Egyptian capital. One marvels at the works constructed here and half believes that the Arabs are right in saying that the old Egyptians were wizards, able to transport mountains of stone at the mere stroke of the enchanter's wand. But the glory of Egypt has departed. Race after race follows the same inevitable cycle of progress, culmination, decadence, decay and death. Egypt, the mother of civilization, has led the way, but none of its successors will leave such vast material vestiges of power, and few can show such proofs of intellectual ability. Standing on the threshold of pre-historic times, it nevertheless reveals to us a people marvellously skilled in astronomical calculations, art and science, and thoroughly convinced of immortality. Of all the countries of Antiquity, therefore, Egypt most charms us by the irresistible attraction of undying fame.

NAZARETH, PALESTINE.—Few Oriental towns are so attractive to look upon as Nazareth, especially in March and April, for then the combination it presents of white-walled houses and bright green foliage is charming. Most of its inhabitants are prosperously engaged in farming, and their costumes are very showy and elaborate. On festal days the women wear gay, embroidered jackets, and have their foreheads and breasts almost covered with coins. The traveller can see in Nazareth the reputed sites of all the events recorded in the Bible as having taken place there. There, for example, is the Church of the Annunciation, supposed to contain the very localities where the angel stood while uttering to Mary his glad tidings, and there Mary herself stood during the Annunciation. Besides this, one may see the site of the Virgin's House; the Workshop of Joseph; the Synagogue in which Christ is said to have taught; and the "Table of Jesus," which is a broad flat rock, on which Christ is said to have dined with his disciples after the resurrection. Whatever may be thought of the authenticity of these places, there is one object just outside the town of whose antiquity there can be no question. It is a copious spring of water gushing from the hillside, and Nazarene women may be constantly seen filling their pitchers with the precious liquid. As this is the only spring that Nazareth possesses, it is almost certain that Mary and the child Jesus must often have resorted thither in much the same way that Syrian mothers and their children visit the place to-day. Jerusalem is of course the supreme point of interest in the Holy Land, but no Christian traveller will omit, if possible, this little town of Nazareth, where Jesus passed his childhood and early manhood, as "He increased in wisdom and stature and in favour with God and man."

GATE TO LUCKNOW, INDIA.—Lucknow is one of the most important cities of India. It has a population of 300,000, and abounds in beautiful specimens of Oriental architecture. In looking on its gates, domes and minarets one is continually reminded of scenes in Cairo and Constantinople. It is also a city of great wealth, and the works of its goldsmiths are famed throughout the world. The name "Lucknow," however, recalls to all English-speaking people very different souvenirs from those of architecture or the art of jewellers. This was in 1857–58 the scene of the awful British massacre, the thrilling story of which can hardly be surpassed in history. Inside of the Residency here were collected about 2,200 persons, of whom over 500 were women and children. Six hundred of them were English soldiers. The rest were natives who had remained faithful. The attacking force numbered 50,000 men. Most of the English there were doomed, but sold their lives as dearly as possible, and actually held out for three months during the appalling heat of an Indian summer! At last the brave General Havelock reached Lucknow and rescued those who survived. The atrocities which the Indians had perpetrated in killing English women and children fairly maddened the victorious troops, and they slaughtered the Sepoys with savage fury. The street represented in the illustration is the one along which Havelock fought his way through the city to the Residency. The great mutiny was put down, but its memory remains, as the lurid glare of a distant conflagration lights up the sky with the red tint of blood.

NATIONAL CONGRESS, SANTIAGO, CHILI.—Santiago, the Chilian capital, is situated near the foot-hills of the Andes, far enough inland from the coast to be safe at least from attacks made from the ocean. Its climate is delightful. The temperature ranges from 52° Fahrenheit in winter to about 75° in summer. Rain falls there only during the four winter months. Many of its public buildings, like this, its Hall of Congress, are exceedingly handsome, and it contains a great number of tasteful and even elegant residences. Santiago has about 190,000 inhabitants, and as most of them are averse to walking, tram-cars are well patronized. The conductors of these public vehicles are *girls*, whose uniform consists of a white apron and a bag for silver coin. They seem to perform their duties modestly and satisfactorily, and this peculiarity of Chilian street life may extend further northward! Most of the buildings have but one story, and are built as lightly as possible for fear of earthquakes; but some more modern structures are made with very thick brick walls and massive stone foundations, while the second story is braced together with iron. There is in Santiago a large and elegant theatre which has a regular opera season and many entertainments given by travelling companies. The Government of Chili is a Republic, and its Constitution is modelled after that of the United States. The President is elected every five years. The legislative power resides in a National Congress, composed of a Chamber of Deputies, elected by the departments in the proportion of one deputy for every 30,000 inhabitants, and of a Senate, whose members are elected by popular vote at the rate of one senator for every three deputies. The judicial power is vested in magistrates appointed by the President.

PASS OF USPALLATA, ANDES MOUNTAINS, SOUTH AMERICA.—To cross the Andes is by no means an easy undertaking. Much of the route is practically through an elevated desert. Bare granite rocks rise on every side and reflect the sun with an angry glare. For a long distance there is no shade, no shelter, and worse than all, no water. The dry dust, loosened by the strong winds, parches the throat and inflames the eyes until one suffers intensely. Scanty shrubs, cactus, and sterile cliffs succeed each other mile after mile in dreary monotony. From time to time one comes upon a camp of engineers engaged in surveying a route for the railway, which, when completed, will be a wonderful triumph of engineering skill. To these camps everything has to be carried on mule-back, even the fodder for the animals themselves. Over this fearful route, however, the telegraph wire goes from the Argentine Republic into Chili, passing the summit of the Andes in underground cables. At the highest part of the pass, nearly 13,000 feet above the level of the sea, some travellers, and even mules and horses, have great difficulty in breathing, owing to the rarefaction of the air. Persons thus affected often bleed at the nose and lungs, and are sometimes compelled to retrace their steps. At times, too, such gales of wind prevail here that men and mules have been blown down precipices to destruction. Every afternoon the wind blows with great violence, and it is considered much safer to cross the crest in the early morning. But to compensate one for these hardships the scenery is frequently grand beyond description, and the descent into the valleys of Chili is enchantingly beautiful.

MONTREAL AND MOUNT ROYAL, CANADA.—Montreal, the commercial metropolis of Canada, is a very attractive city, located on the best situation which the St. Lawrence river offers after Quebec. Its population is about 141,000, of whom 78,000 are of French descent. Of course the French language is very extensively used here. More than one-half the population of Montreal are Roman Catholics. The city is built upon a series of terraces which indicate beyond a doubt the former levels of the river. Its buildings are massive and frequently imposing, and its streets are finely paved. It was not until 1760 that the French power in Canada was finally destroyed by the surrender of Montreal. Since then, though its history has been comparatively uneventful, it has made great material progress in all directions. Still it is not by any means a monotonous and purely commercial town; for the variety here of different races, languages and religions gives to the place a certain rivalry of thought and interest which imparts zest and excitement to otherwise unimportant events. One of the principal features of Montreal is a long wooded ridge behind the city, 750 feet high and covering 430 acres. It is Mount Royal, and was purchased by the Municipal Government for a park in 1874. The view from this precipitous and shaded bluff is beautiful and very extensive, embracing in one direction level, cultivated plains and the distant Adirondack mountains, and in the other the city itself and the lovely valley of the St. Lawrence. The visitor may drive to the summit of Mount Royal, or if inclined to test his muscles, he can walk either up long flights of steps which have been built to the very top, or long paths of easy grade. One singular feature of the mountain is a lake of wonderful clearness, which supplies holy water for the city's Catholic churches.

YOSEMITE VALLEY FROM ARTISTS' POINT, CALIFORNIA.—One never wearies of this inimitable valley. From every "Point" of observation new marvels are discernible. For ages it has made this landscape glorious with its stern, savage cliffs, its barren precipices, its flower-strewn carpet of rich vegetation and its stupendous water-falls. During unnumbered centuries, with her usual sublime indifference to Man's appreciation, Nature displayed these wondrous beauties daily to the passing sun, and nightly to the moon and stars, without a human eye to gaze upon their charms. Then followed other centuries when to the savages who visited this place its marvellous phenomena seemed but the manifestations of some hideous deity, awakening little more appreciation in their minds than could be aroused in the wild beasts which made its caves their homes. But now this grand Yosemite is a kind of shrine, where thousands annually come to worship the Eternal Power which has thus revealed itself. "The undevout astronomer is mad!" exclaimed the poet as he gazed upon the darkened universe strewn with innumerable suns and systems. So may one also characterize the man who treads this mountain-girdled valley of Yosemite, and does not reverently look through Nature up to Nature's God. Anticipate what you will, you never can be disappointed in the Yosemite. In the words of the Queen of Sheba, the astonished traveller here exclaims: "The half has not been told me!" Nor does familiarity with its glories lessen their effect. Truer words were never written than those of Keats, "A thing of beauty is a joy forever;" and whatever else may be forgotten in this crowded life of ours, the vision of this glorious ravine will linger like an inspiration with the traveller who has stood between its peerless walls, till memory shall have lost its power and till his eyes have closed upon the finite to behold the infinite.

EIFFEL TOWER, PARIS.—One of the marvels of the recent Paris Exposition was this light yet massive tower, reaching a height attained by nothing else of human workmanship upon the surface of our globe. Unbounded ridicule was at first heaped upon the architect who dared propose to erect such a construction in the centre of a city which is so beautiful and artistic. Critics declared that such an unsightly object would injure Paris, as much as a positive deformity would a human being. Others maintained that it would be dangerous. Most people thought that it was at least a waste of money. All these predictions failed of verification. The monument was built to a height of 985 feet above the Seine. Far from being a hideous structure, as was prophesied, it is remarkably light, graceful and well proportioned. Nor have any bad results ensued either to the Parisians or to M. Eiffel. During the Exposition nothing was more popular than a trip up the Eiffel Tower, and it proved a "mint of money" to its owners. For the colossal shaft was utilized not merely as a point where glorious views could be obtained, but on the first of its great platforms, 376 feet from the ground, were restaurants and cafés, where several hundred people could be accommodated at one time. The second platform, used chiefly for observation, has a height of 863 feet. That seemed quite high enough to most travellers, but if they wished to complete the ascent they could be transported by elevators over one hundred feet higher still, whence Paris looked like an immense child's-puzzle spread out in dwarf-like figures far below.

GROUP OF MOORISH WOMEN, ALGERIA, AFRICA.—The splendid drama of the Moors, which had held the stage of history for 700 years, ended in 1492, when they were driven out from Spain into Africa. That race has now degenerated, yet occasionally in Morocco and Algeria one sees some Moors whose forms and faces seem not unworthy of their glorious past. A peculiarity of their dwellings even now is the horse-shoe arch, which was represented in the magnificent Mosque of Cordova in Spain and in the courts of the Alhambra. Whether these Moorish homes are happy ones may well be doubted. It is true, life is said to move on quietly in the seclusion of the Harem everywhere in Mohammedan countries, but human nature being much the same the world over, it is probable that tragic scenes sometimes take place there. When a woman truly loves, she must be jealous of her rival; and the dagger, the cup of poisoned coffee, the silken girdle used for purposes of strangulation, are dangerous weapons in the hands of jealousy. Although allowed by law to have four wives, the Moslem of the present day rarely has more than two, partly through motives of economy, partly in accordance with the Oriental proverb (founded probably on experience), that a household with four women is like a vessel in a storm!

DAMASCUS, SYRIA.—The Arabs have long regarded Damascus as a foretaste of Paradise, and have called it exultantly "The joy of the whole earth." In fact to the followers of Mahomet, emerging from the deserts of Arabia, this must have seemed to them the Garden of the Gods. The Roman Emperor, Julian, called it the Eye of the East, Persian and Arabic poets have sung of its beauty in rapturous strains. It appears in the distance like an oasis of dense, luxuriant foliage, from which rise scores of bulbous domes and glittering minarets. Like all Oriental cities, it proves somewhat disenchanting upon close inspection, but its fountains, its stately trees, its air laden with the perfume of unnumbered gardens, its mosques, and its marvellous bazars—all these together make Damascus the rival of Cairo, a place where the jewelled portals of the Orient open wide before us, and all our anticipations of the East are realized. Even the houses, which appear plain and unattractive without, contain apartments of great luxury, with marble-paved courtyards and a profusion of rare flowers, graceful fountains, rich Syrian tapestries, and soft divans upon which rest in voluptuous languor some Eastern women lulled by the murmur of melodious fountains into that dreamy repose so dear to all inhabitants of the Orient. Damascus is one of the oldest cities in the world; so old, that it is useless to try to recount its history here. It has seen many masters. Faith after faith has flourished here, from that of Jove to that of Mahomet. It has lain for ages like a lovely slave in the market-place contended for by wrangling rivals.

COURT OF THE MYRTLES, ALHAMBRA, SPAIN.—This is usually the first apartment of the Moorish palace that the traveller enters, and as by the stroke of some enchanter's wand he seems to have stepped from Europe into Asia. Before him is a marble basin of water, 132 feet in length, now tenanted by goldfish and surrounded by myrtle hedges and orange trees bright with their glistening leaves and fruit of gold. At each extremity of this court are slender marble columns supporting walls and arches which look as delicate as chiselled ivory. Above his head is one of the characteristic roofs of the Alhambra, consisting of countless pieces of cedar wood inlaid with mother-of-pearl, and resembling the cells of a honey-comb, or the roof of a stalactite grotto. So dainty and delicate is the entire court, that it seems almost wrong to walk upon its marble pavement, which is as spotlessly white as when pressed by the feet of the fair Sultanas, for this was the bathing-place of the wives of Caliphs. At the right and left of the illustration we see prettily carved mural apertures, in which it is supposed the Sultanas left their slippers when they went to bathe, or which held the exquisite Alhambra vases, some of which have been discovered here. It seems impossible that this enchanting palace has not been occupied for centuries. Every part of it seems merely awaiting the return of some Princess of the Arabian Nights. At each end of this basin we see the base of a fountain, usually of alabaster, filling the air with freshness and the continual cadence of a song.

STATUE OF LEONARDO DA VINCI, MILAN, ITALY.—Almost in the shadow of the grand Milan Cathedral rises this noble monument in marble, erected in 1872 to the memory of that immortal artist of the Renaissance, Leonardo da Vinci. Upon a lofty pedestal stands the colossal statue of the master, apparently absorbed in thought. Below him are life-size figures of four of his pupils, and copies in relief of some of his principal works. The city of Milan has done well to honour thus the most versatile of men ; for it was here that he exhibited his brilliant talents to an astonishing degree under the patronage of the Milanese Duke. Here he lived nearly twenty years. Here in the convent of the Madonna delle Grazie is the ruin of his wonderful masterpiece, "The Last Supper," with which the world has long since been made familiar through paintings and engravings. There seems to have been no department of art in which this extraordinary Leonardo did not excel, for he was famous as a painter, sculptor, architect, engineer, musician, poet and manager of all the gaieties of the Ducal court ! Beyond this monument of Da Vinci the illustration gives us a hint of the spacious and beautiful Gallery of Victor Emanuel. It is in the form of a Latin cross, with an octagon in the centre, and is about 1,000 feet in length and 24 feet high. It forms a most attractive promenade, for not only does it contain many cafés and handsome shops, but its decorations are extremely rich and elegant. No less than twenty-four statues of famous Italians adorn its walls, and many elaborate frescoes also claim one's admiration.

CLIMBING THE GREAT PYRAMID, EGYPT.—Once these stupendous mountains of stone could not be climbed. They were covered with a smooth porcelain-like coating and presented an enamelled appearance. But this substance and many of the huge stones of the Pyramids were long since carried off to Cairo for building materials, and now therefore tourists make the ascent of the great Pyramid "Cheops," using the broken surface as a kind of staircase. It is no easy task ; but Arabs are always ready to pull and to push, and whenever the traveller is weary and seats himself, they will rub his limbs and back, praise his strength and courage. In about fifteen minutes one can thus reach the summit of Cheops, which is now a platform about thirty feet square. Only by actually making the ascent and looking down upon its vast receding walls can one appreciate the vastness of this Pyramid and realize what an amount of human labour must have been expended in its construction ; for he then bears in mind that all this mountain beneath him is *a solid mass of masonry*, with the exception of the narrow galleries leading to the King's and Queen's apartments. Such a stupendous production therefore compels him to think with additional wonder and reverence on the marvellous civilization which flourished here six thousand years ago beside the Nile, and must even then have been existing here for a very long period in order to have attained to achievements in architecture such as the astonished world has never equalled since.

THE "HOLY NIGHT," (By CORREGGIO), DRESDEN GALLERY.—Its especial charm is the wonderful light which floods the entire foreground of the scene and emanates from the person of the Divine Child. This radiance falls at first upon the face of the enraptured Mother as she bends in ecstacy over her first-born. Then it lights up an attendant shepherdess, then Joseph in the distance, and finally the angels hovering above the manger, as if unwilling to depart. This work was completed in 1527, and he was miserably compensated for such a masterpiece, having received for it only about eight pounds! No painter save Raphael is considered his equal in depicting sweetness and loveliness, especially in children, while in his treatment of light and shade he is unrivalled. He appears to have been singularly free from jealousy, and was enthusiastic over the productions of other great artists. All the world knows his famous sentence, uttered when he beheld the "Saint Cecilia," of Raphael, and felt the inspiration of that noble work, as he exclaimed in pride and joy, "I also am a painter!" It is impossible to here enumerate all of Correggio's works, some of which rival even the "Holy Night," in beauty; but his "Reading Magdalen," also in the Dresden Gallery, is one of the most exquisite of artistic creations, and justifies the words of the great Venetian genius, when, after looking at some of Correggio's paintings, he exclaimed, "Were I not Titian, I should wish to be Correggio!"

ROSENBERG PALACE, COPENHAGEN, DENMARK.—This singular edifice is no longer an abode of Royalty, but serves now as a National Museum, containing many interesting relics of the Danish dynasties. A visit to it calls to mind the prominent part which little Denmark has assumed in History. For, although insignificant *now*, the time has been when Europe trembled at her fleet, and feared her as the most piratical of nations. For centuries she ruled all Scandinavia, bearing upon a single shield the crowns of Denmark, Sweden and Norway ; while we cannot forget that Denmark conquered England, and that a line of Danish Kings once occupied the throne now held by Queen Victoria. Moreover, though this kingdom has now little strength in respect to fleets and armies, Denmark is nevertheless astonishingly strong in having allied itself by marriage with most of the leading nations of the world. One daughter of the King of Denmark, for example, is married to the Prince of Wales, and thus in all probability is destined to be Queen of England and Empress of India. Another, as the wife of the Czar, is to-day Empress of all the Russias. As for the sons, the eldest married the daughter of the King of Sweden ; the second son is King of the Greeks and husband of Olga, the most beautiful princess of the Russian court ; while other children still remain to form perhaps yet other strong alliances !

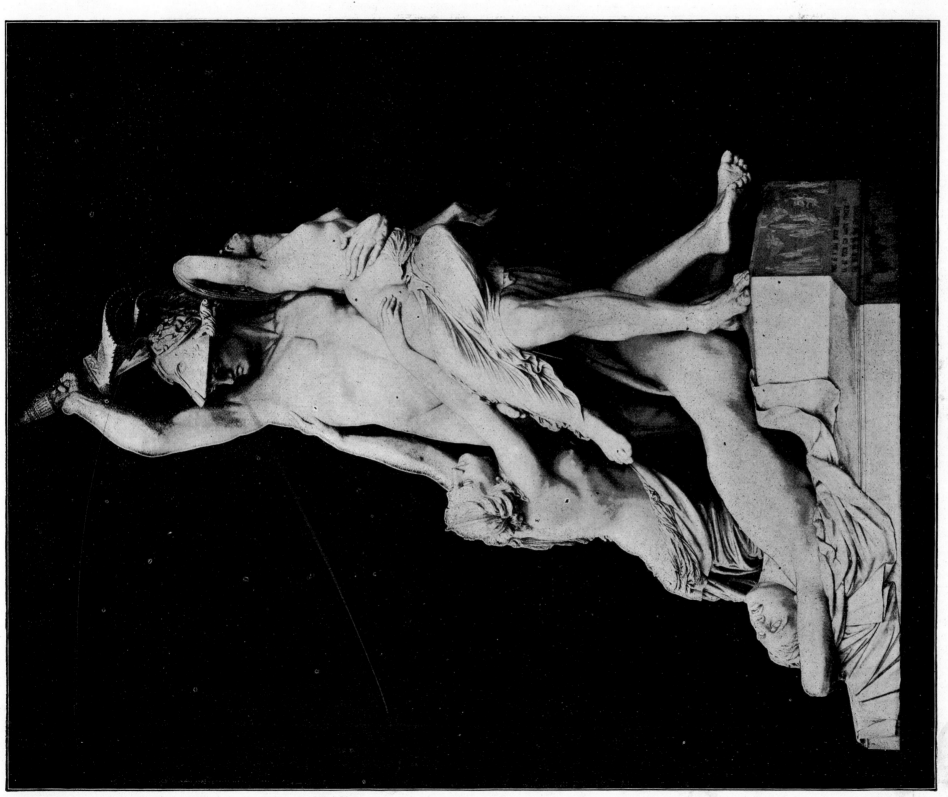

SEIZURE OF POLYXENA (By Fedi) FLORENCE.—Prominent among the works of art in the historic Loggia, or Portico, of Florence, is a group which makes upon the traveller a profound impression. It is a modern work by the Florentine sculptor, Fedi, completed in 1865. Our admiration of it increases when we learn that, large and complicated as it is, all its four figures were produced from *a single block of Carrara marble!* Before this was achieved the sculptor Fedi was unknown, toiling in poverty. But having once produced this, with a single bound he sprang into celebrity, and this, his masterpiece, was placed here in the Portico, as on a throne of honour, among the statues of Cellini, Donatello, and John of Bologna. Moreover, so jealous was the city of her new possession that she made Fedi promise never to repeat the group. It represents a painful subject of mythology, the seizure of Polyxena by Pyrrhus. The conqueror, whose form is a magnificent combination of strength and beauty, is bearing off the captured girl, while at his feet lies in the agony of death the maiden's brother, who has tried in vain to rescue her. Beside him, and still clinging to her child with trembling hands, we see the mother, Hecuba, whose face and attitude are worthy of high praise. As for the girl, her form is wonderfully beautiful, none of its rounded outlines being lost beneath the drapery, creased by her struggles in a thousand folds. Each time one passes the Loggia during his stay in Florence, he always looks with undiminished pleasure at this noble work.

THE GREAT BRONZE BUDDHA, JAPAN.—Kamakura, once the capital of Eastern Japan, has now sunk into a sea-side village, which is a famous health resort for the Yokohama residents. The chief sight there is the colossal bronze deity represented in this illustration. This "Great Buddha" stands unique among Japanese works of art. To be fully appreciated it must be visited many times. There was a temple in this place as early as the eighth century, but this image is of much later date. Its precise history is involved in obscurity. Tradition, however, says that Yoritomo, a famous Japanese king and warrior, when taking part in the dedication of a great statue at Nara, conceived the desire of having a similar object of worship at his own capital, but died before he could put the plan into execution. One of the ladies of his court undertook to collect funds for the purpose, and in the year 1252 the Kamakura "Buddha" was cast in bronze by Ono Goroemon. The statue is best seen from about half-way up the approach. Its dimensions are approximately as follows: Height, 49 feet 7 inches; circumference, 97 feet 2 inches; length of face, 8 feet 5 inches; length of eye, 3 feet 11 inches; length of nose, 3 feet 9 inches. The eyes are of pure gold, and the silver boss weighs 30 pounds. The image is formed of sheets of bronze cast separately, brazed together and finished off on the outside with the chisel. The hollow interior of the image contains a small shrine and the visitor may ascend into the head.

TOWN HALL AND SQUARE, SYDNEY, AUSTRALIA.—Sydney is a charmingly located city. Its harbour is one of the most beautiful in the world, entered as it is through an imposing gateway flanked on each side by precipitous cliffs, known respectively as "North Head" and "South Head," while another rock called "Middle Head" stands in the centre, apparently blocking up the way. Around the harbour of Sydney are charming bits of rocky or sylvan scenery, and on many wooded promontories can be seen the villas of the wealthy. The city of Sydney is on some accounts more attractive than Melbourne, and has many handsome buildings. In its vicinity are many handsome residences, elegantly furnished and surrounded by extensive and beautifully-kept grounds. The principal exports of Sydney are tallow, hides, wool and gold. The last named article has an annual value of about one million pounds. Of course one who lives in the civilized portions of Australia and in such cities as Sydney and Melbourne, has no more idea of the Australian aborigines in the interior of the continent than most Americans have of the Indians in the "Far West." Nevertheless, they exist there, though they are now rapidly dying out in the presence of a superior race. They are much lower in the scale of humanity than the natives of New Zealand, being naturally savages of the lowest kind, absolutely naked, ignorant of the use of all metals, having no houses, and rarely attempting to cultivate the ground. But in the course of time these aborigines will inevitably fade away, and the civilization represented here at Sydney will characterize all the mighty area of Australia.

THE BUILDING OF THE PYRAMIDS, MUNICH, GERMANY (By Gustav Richter).—One of the finest paintings of the modern German school is this by Gustav Richter (born in Berlin in 1822), famous for his rich effects of colour as well as for his admirable drawing. It represents a Pharaoh watching with pride and satisfaction the erection of one of those stupendous mountains of stone, which rear their awful forms beside the Nile, just on the edge of the mighty Desert of Sahara. These pyramids were the colossal sepulchres of Kings; the most enormous ever reared by perishable man. When a Pharaoh ascended the throne, he began at once the construction of his tomb, usually in the form of a pyramid. The longer he reigned, the larger grew the Pyramid. He watched its growth either thus close at hand, or from his palace in the neighbouring city of Memphis, whose funeral monuments have thus outlived its stately palaces and temples. The whole region along the edge of the Desert for twenty-five miles was the cemetery of Memphis, and the ground is honey-combed with sepulchres, and covered with many pyramids in various stages of perfection, preservation and magnitude. Pyramid-building was common here as late as the coming of Abraham into Egypt, about 2,000 years before Christ; but later, when the capital had been removed up the Nile from Memphis to Thebes, rock-hewn tombs seem to have been preferred.

COURTYARD OF THE DUCAL PALACE, VENICE.—In another illustration the exterior of this wonderful building is portrayed, as it fronts upon the Piazzetta. We are here looking on a portion of its inner courtyard, around which rise the marble walls of the Palace, magnificently decorated with stone carving and statuary in bronze and marble. In the foreground is one of two elaborate bronze well-curbs here, the work of Venetian artists 350 years ago. Upon their marble steps Venetian women often sit to rest themselves before returning homeward with their pails of water, gossiping gaily of to-day, unmindful of the history with which each stone in this old building seems at times so eloquent. In the distance we perceive the marble steps, known as the "Giants' Staircase," because of the colossal statues of Mars and Neptune which decorate its summit. This is more than 400 years old, and for centuries at the head of its steps the Doges of Venice were crowned. Byron in his tragedy of "Marino Faliero" makes this the place of that sovereign's execution, and the concluding line of his drama is, "The gory head rolls down the Giants' Steps." Unfortunately, Marino Faliero was decapitated before this stairway had been built, but it is a fact that he was beheaded in this palace. Just beyond the "Giants' Steps" is a flight of stairs leading to the upper story, called the "Scala d'Oro," or the "Golden Staircase," from the magnificence of its ornamentation.

GLACIER POINT, YOSEMITE VALLEY, CALIFORNIA.—If possible, all visitors to the Yosemite should make an excursion around it on the outside of the valley itself. Such a tour can now be safely accomplished on horseback over beaten trails, and the circuit of the Yosemite can thus be made in a few days, the memory of which will be well worth a year of ordinary existence. Even those who can not make the entire excursion should at least ride out on the "McCauley trail" a few miles, as far as "Glacier Point," which is a stupendous, perpendicular mountain of solid rock more than 3,000 feet in height. The bottom of the valley, which is one vast flower-garden, looks like a long and narrow Persian rug of varied hues, on which occasional structures, even when viewed through a field-glass, seem like dice upon a checker-board, while trees of several centuries' growth appear at that distance no larger than tacks. Directly opposite, along the front of a gigantic mountain a mile and a half away, the glorious Yosemite Fall comes plunging downward for 2,600 feet in three prodigious leaps, of which the first alone clears 1,500 feet! No falls in the world, not even in Norway, equal this in height and grandeur, and the solemn and eternal roar of its descending waters seems to the lonely tourist on Glacier Point like some unearthly, awe-inspiring symphony, descriptive of the Worship of Humanity on one of the grandest altars of God's Universe.

GRAND OPERA HOUSE, PARIS.—This is not merely one of the most magnificent structures of the French metropolis, but is the largest theatre in the world; not strictly so in regard to its seating capacity, which accommodates about 2,200 people, but in the area of three acres which it occupies in the very heart of the city. The first view of it as one approaches it along the Boulevards can never be forgotten. Broad marble steps lead up to a façade adorned with groups of statuary representing Lyric Poetry, Idyllic Poetry, Music, Declamation, Song and Dance. Above these are medallions of four great composers, and over these extends along the full width of the structure a Loggia or gallery, embellished with beautiful Corinthian monolithic columns and a marble parapet. Above the windows of this Loggia the eye beholds with pleasure medallion busts, in gilded bronze, of Mozart, Beethoven, Auber, Rossini, Meyerbeer and Halevy, whose noble works are heard so frequently within the Temple of Music, which they thus adorn. To right and left upon the roof colossal groups in gilded bronze stand radiantly forth against the sky, portraying the divinities of Poetry and Music, with the muses in their train. While, to complete the charm of this extraordinary building, there rises in the centre a majestic dome above the crown of which we see, triumphant over all, the statue of Apollo holding aloft a golden lyre, which still reflects the splendour of the setting sun long after evening has begun to spread its shadows over the adjacent streets, which soon will burst forth from that temporary twilight into a blaze of artificial brilliancy almost as light as day, which makes the place of the Grand Opera seem like the diamond-clasp in that long belt of gaiety, display and fashion known as the Parisian Boulevards.

CHURCHYARD OF STOKE-POGIS, ENGLAND.—To this lovely churchyard the matchless "Elegy" by Gray has given an immortal charm. The place has altered little since the poet's time, save that "yon ivy-mantled tower," which he described is now surmounted by a modern spire. It seems unsuited to the place, and the ivy (while clinging lovingly to the old wall) avoids the spire as if it were a strange intruder. But this aside, the place is as it was when the poet lingered here at sunset, as "The curfew tolled the knell of parting day!" Beneath its oriel window rich with ivy is the poet's grave. What an ideal resting-place for one who has identified his name forever with its peaceful beauty! Standing here, what added significance and pathos are given to his lines:

"Beneath those rugged elms, that yew-tree's shade,
    Where heaves the turf in many a mouldering heap,
Each in his narrow cell forever laid,
    The rude forefathers of the hamlet sleep.

"Perhaps in this neglected spot is laid
    Some heart once pregnant with celestial fire,
Hands that the rod of empire might have swayed,
    Or waked to ecstacy the living lyre.

"Full many a gem of purest ray serene,
    The dark, unfathomed caves of ocean bear;
Full many a flower is born to blush unseen,
    And waste its sweetness on the desert air."

HOUSES OF PARLIAMENT, VIENNA.—The visitor to Vienna twenty-five years ago would hardly recognize the city now. It has been wonderfully embellished and improved by the completion of the "Ring Strassen," namely, a series of Boulevards two miles in length enclosing old Vienna like a ring or belt. The original city of the Hapsburgs was formerly surrounded by a moat and fortified wall; but gradually the expansive force within the town overleaped those barriers, and finally, in 1858, those ramparts were blown up and levelled; the moat was filled; and on the curving terrace thus created this line of boulevards was made, dividing old and new Vienna, and thus resembling a girdle of surpassing beauty. Moreover, the traveller now beholds with admiration and astonishment (like precious jewels in this splendid girdle), a constant series of imposing structures, all of them handsome, most of them majestic and ranking certainly among the finest edifices in the world. Among them are these New Houses of Parliament, recently completed at a cost of several millions. Their general plan is not unlike that of the American legislative halls at Washington. The Senate House is on the right; the Chamber of Deputies upon the left; each one an independent building, richly adorned with marble statues and beautiful reliefs, and on the various corners with colossal chariots of Victory in bronze.

THE FORUM, POMPEII.—Notwithstanding all that we may have read about Pompeii, to walk among its excavated streets and temples is an unique and never-to-be-forgotten experience, surpassing all one's anticipations. For here beneath the awful mount, which still holds high its smoking torch, lies an ancient Roman city, partially ruined, it is true, but so protected from the Goths and Vandals by its very lava shroud, that now in looking on its streets and buildings we can imagine them re-peopled, and realize how life went on beneath this same blue sky when Jesus walked in Galilee. Here are frescoes undimmed by the fatal touch of time. Here have been found scores of dead bodies and gems which fell from the trembling hands of those who fled in terror. The walls, though roofless, are still standing firmly. The columns have not lost their colour. This Forum of Pompeii had not been quite completed when the destruction of the city came, and these, its numerous pedestals for statues, were for the most part unoccupied when the deadly ashes fell, to wrap them in a winding sheet, which only in this nineteenth century has been removed. Pompeii was a favourite summer-resort of wealthy Romans. Cicero had a villa there and was very fond of the place. The fatal catastrophe occurred on the 24th of August, A. D. 79, when Pompeii was buried in showers of ashes and red-hot pumice stones to a depth of twenty feet. Much more of the city still remains to be excavated. The Government allows £2,500 a year for the work to go on.

STREET IN TOKIO, JAPAN.—Tokio (formerly called Yedo) is the capital of Japan, and is an hour's ride by rail from Yokohama. It was thrown open to foreign travel only as recently as 1869, but it has made up for lost time by assuming many European characteristics. It now has numerous buildings constructed on the European style. Foreign dress and the European mode of arranging the hair have also been very extensively adopted. Electric lights and telephones no longer excite wonder here. Tram-cars and omnibusses may be also seen, although the vehicle most used is the *Jinrikisha*, specimens of which are visible at the left of this illustration. In these a *man* places himself between the shafts and plays the part of a horse for as many hours and for as long a distance as the traveller can bear to be drawn by him. The size of Tokio is enormous, almost equalling that of London, and its population is nearly one and a half millions. The "sights" of such a city, as may be easily imagined, can not be exhausted so soon as the sight-seer himself. Numerous and interesting temples, the Mikado's Palace, the Imperial University, the Arsenal, the famous Ueno Park, the admirable Museum of Japanese Antiquities, these together with the fascinating shops of Curios, Lacquer Work and Bronzes, furnish material for many days of constant pleasure and employment. There are few sidewalks in Tokio, the streets themselves being used freely, and not without danger, by foot-passengers and vehicles. Every omnibus and coaches of all descriptions carry horns, which the drivers blow to warn people to clear the way. Extensive conflagrations frequently take place here, for most of the buildings are made of wood. Earthquakes are of common occurrence, and have occasioned at times enormous loss of life.

VALPARAISO HARBOUR, CHILI.—Santiago, the capital of Chili, lies inland about a hundred miles from Valparaiso, which is its celebrated sea-port. The Bay of Valparaiso, although containing always a multitude of steamers, iron-clads, sailing ships and smaller craft, is by no means an ideal one. It is very dangerously exposed to northern winds, but is provided with a fine Mole furnished with excellent hydraulic machinery for unloading ships from foreign lands. A long sweep of quays is formed about the curving shore by an immense sea-wall. Near the Mole are the extensive buildings of the Custom-house and bonded warehouses. From the harbour the city climbs inland up the hills, terrace above terrace. Valparaiso is considered to be quite an English town. At all events English ships are always floating in its bay. The English tongue is heard continually upon its streets. A number of its inns have such emphatically British names as "The Queen's Arms" and the "Red Lion." German influence is also felt very strongly here. The truth is that European capital has been so lavishly invested in Chili, that European agents must come here to look after it. Busy with the development of our own enormously productive country, we have had in the United States only a faint idea of the natural resources of the South American republics. Foreigners, however, have long since discovered these, and now in almost every port along the coast of Chili can be found colonies of English and Germans, managing great business enterprises and accumulating fortunes rapidly. Until recently the Chilians themselves have not engaged in large commercial schemes. Some of them have made enormous fortunes in mining, but as a rule they are content with an easy life of pleasure, and allow foreign capital and enterprise to open up and utilize the natural riches of their country.

ROYAL PALACE, HONOLULU, SANDWICH ISLANDS.—If this residence of the ruler of the Sandwich Islands appears plain and unpretending, we have only to recall the fact that Honolulu harbour was discovered only a hundred years ago (1794) by Captain Brown, who was promptly murdered by the natives. Great changes have certainly taken place here in a century! The contrast between this palace of the late King Kalakua and the hut of one of his royal ancestors is as remarkable as that between the palace of the German Emperor and this abode of royalty in Honolulu. Some members of the royal family are visible in this illustration at the left. King Kalakua stands beside the lofty palm tree, and near him are his wife and daughter. In the rear is seen Col. Judd, his Secretary of State. If "Divinity doth hedge a King" in these days of Democracy, a tailor must help make the king divine. A uniform, even though it be a semi-civilized one, is more imposing than a plain sack coat, and a diadem, even if it be of feathers, is preferable, for a monarch, to a straw hat, such as are worn by all the world besides. A broad piazza entirely surrounds this palace. Its chief apartment is that wherein the throne was placed, and where the royal levees were held. Honolulu itself has a population of about 14,000 souls. The buildings consist largely of one-story wooden houses, mingled with grass huts embowered in luxuriant foliage. Still it has several churches, hotels and public buildings of some architectural beauty. Its streets are straight and clean. Charming tropical scenery abounds; and there is always pleasant foreign society here, chiefly English and American. Honolulu can not be called isolated from the world, for steamers run thence to San Francisco, Australia, England, New York, Germany, China and Peru.

MOSQUE OF OMAR, JERUSALEM.—Jerusalem, the sacred city of the Jews, and the holy city of the Christians, is also now a place of pilgrimage to the followers of Mahomet. For more than 1,000 years it has been in the possession of the Moslems, and this magnificent Mosque of Omar is to them a place second in sanctity only to Mecca itself. This Mosque is built in the form of an octagon, each side being sixty-six feet long. The lower part is of white marble, the upper part is covered with porcelain tiles, whose colours intersect each other in beautiful designs. Passages from the Koran are also interwoven with this decoration. Unlike most Mosques, no tapering minarets rise from this towards heaven. Its elegantly proportioned dome was thought to be sufficient. In fact, it is so light and graceful that from a distance one could easily expect to see it float away in the blue air, like a balloon of silk. This structure covers the site of Solomon's Temple, and beneath the dome is the "Sacred Rock," the natural summit of Mt. Moriah, and probably the foundation for the sacrificial altar of the Jews, in their splendid shrine. The Moslems greatly revere this rock, for Mahomet is believed to have there knelt in prayer, and to have ascended thence to Heaven. He derived most of his religious ideas from the Jews, and venerated this part of Jerusalem, as having been hallowed by the prayers of Hebrew patriarchs. Few places in the world, therefore, are more revered than the eminence on which this Mosque now stands, and few historic shrines are so deserving of respectful interest.

AQUEDUCT NEAR QUERETARO, MEXICO.—A little distance from the pretty city of Queretaro in Mexico, the Mexican Central Railroad passes beneath a fine stone aqueduct which was built in 1738 by the Spaniards at a cost of $125,000. Of this sum, about $82,000 was contributed by one private individual! It conveys to the city clear spring water, the source of which is in the mountains five miles away. The water is at first brought through a tunnel, and finally makes its triumphal entry into Queretaro over seventy-four of these arches, the highest of which is ninety-two feet above the ground. The water supply of the city is thereby rendered ample and wholesome, and there are more than twenty fountains within its limits. Queretaro itself is one of the prettiest of Mexican towns, containing nearly 50,000 inhabitants, and situated about 6,000 feet above the level of the sea. It was here that the short-lived Emperor, Maximilian, was betrayed and arrested in 1867, and on a little eminence near the town, on the 19th of June that same year, he was shot by order of the Government, together with his two leading generals, Miramon and Mehia. Upon that hill are now three columns marking the places where the unfortunate trio fell. Maximilian's body was subsequently sent back to Europe in the same ship which, only three years before, had brought him and his beautiful young wife, "Poor Carlotta," out to Mexico, in perfect health and with high hopes of founding here a new and glorious dynasty. Here also in 1848 the treaty of peace between Mexico and the United States was ratified.

THE TROCADERO, PARIS.—Every public building in Paris is not only beautifully situated, but beautiful in itself. This is emphatically true of the Trocadero Palace, an edifice erected for the great Paris Exhibition of 1878. The place which it occupies was long known as one of the most unsightly spots near Paris, having been the site of several stone quarries. But like so many other points in and about the city, it was transformed into a beautiful locality by order of Napoleon III. to whom, with all his faults, Paris is much indebted. The Trocadero itself, with its extensive wings or galleries, occupies a space on the top of a hill 1,300 feet long. It is an immense circular structure crowned by a colossal statue of Fame and flanked on each side by a graceful tower 290 feet high. In front of the whole building is an arcade forming from end to end an unbroken promenade. Below this is a lovely garden, adorned not merely with flower-beds, summer-houses and grottos, but with fountains, of which the finest is a grand cascade 196 feet in diameter, which, when illuminated, as it sometimes is at night by electricity, forms an enchanting spectacle. The Trocadero contains a grand concert hall capable of seating seven thousand people, and its organ is one of the largest in the world. Here are also several museums of great value, among them one portraying different styles of architecture in France, and representing by plaster casts the beautiful portals of the old French cathedrals, the staircases of the French chateaux and the sculptured ornaments of the various Hotels de Ville in French cities. The name of this handsome edifice is derived from one of the forts of Cadiz, Spain, captured by the French in 1823.

BALMORAL CASTLE, SCOTLAND.—This Highland home of Queen Victoria is beautifully situated beside the river Dee some fifty miles from Aberdeen. In her Majesty's absence, the castle is shown to visitors only on the presentation of a written order. The property consists of about 10,000 acres, which belonged formerly to the Earl of Fife, but which, in 1852, became the property of the Crown by the payment of £32,000. The castle itself, which is of light Scotch granite, was erected by the Prince Consort at his own expense. Near by is the Crathie Church, where the Queen attends divine service; and a mile and a half away is Abergeldie Castle, a favourite "Shooting-box" and summer residence of the Prince of Wales. The adjoining country is of great beauty, and the Castle itself resembles a gem in a most attractive setting. At one end of the building is an exceedingly picturesque tower about 100 feet in height, commanding an enchanting view. More than 100 persons can at one time be comfortably lodged in "Balmoral," and it has frequently been the scene of regal hospitality. There can be, it would seem, no difficulty in entertaining visitors here, for within a pistol shot of the Castle is the "bonny river Dee," which sweeps from the Grampian Hills, and whose whole course of ninety miles offers a constant series of delightful views. The neighbourhood also abounds in opportunities not merely for hunting, but for enjoyable excursions among the Highlands, particularly to that grand old mountain Lochnagar, 3,800 feet high, celebrated by the poetry of Lord Byron, and called by the Queen her "Mountain Jewel." From its summit, fully one-half of Scotland is outspread before the vision of the enraptured traveller.

THE RHINE, GUTENFELS AND THE PFALZ, GERMANY.—The interest which we take in the rivers of our globe increases in proportion to the historic souvenirs which seem to mingle with their foam and murmur with their waves. In this sense one of the very foremost of the world's great rivers is the noble Rhine. This illustration reveals to us one of the many ruined castles which from their mountain crests look sadly down upon us as we sail along; their massive walls and ivy-covered battlements telling us of some famous deeds of chivalry or romance through a line of centuries. This castle of Gutenfels owes its title to a lovely maiden named Guta, who was wooed and married by a brave English knight under romantic circumstances which can not be enumerated in this limited space. Below this castle stands in the middle of the Rhine a tower, known as the Pfalz. This tower also has its poetic legend. A certain Count Palatine used this as a prison for his daughter, lest she should marry against his will the hero of her love. But all in vain. The Romeo of the Rhine at last secured admission here disguised as a pilgrim, and the lovers were united in marriage despite all obstacles. It was at this point that the Prussian army under Blucher crossed the Rhine in 1814, to advance on Paris in company with the allied European forces to crush the first Napoleon.

OLD CURIOSITY SHOP, LONDON.—Charles Dickens, in the realm of fiction, has given to the English-reading world a host of veritable *friends*. The heroes of most other novelists amuse, instruct or entertain us, but quickly fade into oblivion, like chance acquaintances. But to the genuine lover of *Dickens* his characters are not fictitious—they are *real*. We laugh with them, we cry with them, we love their virtues, we forgive their frailties, till they are sealed to us as life-long friends. Nor is this all; for Dickens' *characters* are usually linked to certain *places* which he selected with great care, and sketched with wonderful fidelity. It is in fact this vivid picturing of *place and person* that makes it a continual pleasure to trace his works in that great World's Metropolis, of which he was so fond. Thus, of late years, books have been written for this special purpose, and by the aid of these we may spend days in London itself, to say nothing of rural England, noting all sorts of odd localities, streets, houses, inns and churches, such as the quaint sign which suggested to Dickens his idea of Little Nell's "Old Curiosity Shop," to the house where Mr. Tulkinghorn resided, or even the churchyard gate, beside which lay the lifeless body of poor Lady Dedlock. "Charles Dickens' London," therefore, and "Through England with Dickens," should never be omitted from the library of any European tourist who loves the creator of "David Copperfield," "Little Dorrit," and the immortal "Pickwick."

PALACE OF VERSAILLES, FRANCE.—This wonderful building with its extensive park was the home of Louis XIV., who caused it to be erected here at a cost of forty million pounds sterling. The stories of the number of men and horses employed in its construction border on the fabulous. Voltaire called it the "Abyss of Expenses." Here the "Grand Monarch," Louis XIV., died, to be succeeded by the dissolute Louis XV., who also died here, deserted alike by friends and courtiers, as his disease was a malignant form of small-pox. Then for a few years it formed the abode of the ill-fated Louis XVI. and Marie Antoinette, and here at the outbreak of the French Revolution occurred some fearful scenes of violence. Within the great courtyard in the foreground gathered the mob of starving men and women who finally burst into the palace, attempted to kill the Queen, and finally forced the royal family to go back with them to Paris, under the names of "The Baker, the Baker's wife and the Baker's boy." Since that period it has remained practically uninhabited. It is now really a National Museum, containing many interesting historic relics and superb galleries of paintings. At the time of the siege of Paris by the Germans in the Franco-Prussian war, this palace was the headquarters of the Prussian King, and here, on the 18th of January, 1871, he was saluted as Emperor of Germany.

MEISSONIER (JEAN-LOUIS-ERNEST)

NAPOLEON III., AT SOLFERINO, LUXEMBOURG GALLERY, PARIS.—Among the military paintings in the splendid picture gallery of the Luxembourg, in Paris, is this by the famous artist Meissonier, which represents Napoleon III. at Solferino, that little village of northern Italy, which on the 24th of June, 1859, inscribed its name in letters of blood upon the page of history. The combatants were Austria on one side and France and Sardinia on the other; their respective leaders being Franz Joseph, Louis Napoleon and Victor Emanuel. It was a desperate battle, lasting sixteen hours. The Austrian troops as usual fought well, but were as usual defeated. There seems to be a strange fatality in Austrian campaigns. Is it due to the incapacity of Austrian generals? Two weeks later Napoleon III. met the defeated Austrian Emperor at Villafranca and there agreed to preliminaries of peace, which seemed a little tame after this victory of Solferino, and were a crushing blow to those whose hopes had been aroused by Napoleon's famous words, "Italy must be free from the Alps to the Adriatic." For Venice and a part of Lombardy were still left to Austria. Nevertheless, when Napoleon III. sat, as this painting represents him, surveying the victory at Solferino, his star was really at its zenith. Could he have then foreseen the future, he would have sought death on the battlefield; for that was the time for him to die. He would have thus been spared the shame of Mexico, the horrible humiliation of Sedan, and the melancholy death in exile at Chiselhurst. But destiny stood behind him smiling sarcastically even in this hour of triumph. The ancients were right when they said that one of man's greatest misfortunes is that he does not know the right time for him to leave the world!

MISSION OF SAN JUAN, CALIFORNIA.—Ever since the command was given, "Go ye into all the world and preach the Gospel to every creature," there have never been wanting faithful and heroic followers of Christ who have left home, kindred, luxuries and comforts, and have risked their lives unhesitatingly for the salvation of their fellow-men. The history of Catholic Missions among the Indians of California is a very interesting one. If properly described, it would prove as exciting as a romance. The theme has been occasionally touched upon in fiction, and never more gracefully and effectively than the novel called "Ramona," by "H. H." One of these Californian Mission Stations is that of San Juan, outlined in this illustration. It was founded in 1776 in a lovely spot, commanding a charming vista of the blue sea dotted here and there with snowy sails. It was once very prosperous and influential. Some of the Fathers cultivated the vine here with great success. The Indian converts, too, connected with this mission, had an excellent reputation for sincerity and good conduct. At the death of its founder it numbered 470 Christians, and afterwards the number increased so rapidly that in three months there were more natives baptized than during the three previous years. But now San Juan is in a dilapidated condition, and like so many other missions in the United States, its glory has departed with the departure of the Indians themselves. There still remain here, however, the ruins of an immense and handsome church, which was destroyed by an earthquake in 1812, when many Indians were buried in its fall.

RACHEL'S TOMB, NEAR BETHLEHEM, PALESTINE.—On the road between Jerusalem and Bethlehem (a journey which occupies about an hour and a half on horseback) stands a structure known as "Rachel's Tomb." It is revered alike by Christians, Moslems and Jews, and many pilgrims go to it, to pray beneath its dome and to inscribe their names upon its walls. Like almost all the "sacred places" in the Holy Land there is some uncertainty in regard to this. We read in the thirty-fifth chapter of Genesis that, while on her way to Bethlehem, Rachel died in giving birth to Benjamin, and was buried on the road thither. This situation corresponds therefore to the Biblical narrative, and ever since the time of Christ, tradition has always declared it to be the burial-place of Jacob's beloved wife. For many years the site was marked by a pyramid of stones, but in the fifteenth century the monument was changed, and since then has been frequently restored. Those who do not believe that this is Rachel's tomb base their scepticism on the second verse of the tenth chapter of the first book of Samuel. The sepulchre of Rachel is there described as being on the border of the territory of Benjamin, and it is argued that the boundary line between Judah and Benjamin could not have been at this point. A few minutes' walk from this reputed burial-place of Rachel brings the traveller to Bethlehem itself, one of the most sacred and interesting of all localities connected with the Bible.

PROMENADE, NICE, FRANCE.—Nice is the Winter Paradise for invalids and a lovely pleasure-resort for the robust. With a full exposure to the south, and with an amphitheatre of mountains behind to shelter it from the northern winds, we can easily understand the mildness of its climate. In fact its delightful situation led Greek colonists more than 2,000 years ago to choose this for a residence; and from the victory gained here by them over its barbarian defenders, the place was called Nikaia, from which is derived the modern name, *Nice*. Here many fine hotels, charming villas, and a great number of "Pensions," which in the summer time are dark and utterly deserted, become in winter radiant with gas and crowded with humanity. Before the promenade gay parties of excursionists are constantly sailing out in pleasure-boats upon the mirror-like expanse. It is perhaps from the number and the beauty of these fair mariners that this Gulf of Nice is called the "Bay of Angels!" Here also the gay world of fashion displays its brilliant panorama, each winter more bewildering than the last; for while northern climes are shivering in snow and ice, Nice forms a favourite rendezvous not merely for the delicate who come here to beg of Death the respite of a few more months, but also for pleasure-seekers from all portions of the world, especially for subjects of the Czar, who, when they can, are glad to escape the rigour of their northern winters. One of the quays of Nice is named after Napoleon's famous marshal, Massena, who was born here. Here also the immortal patriot Garibaldi first saw the light; here the world-renowned violinist Paganini breathed his last, and now upon a sunny hillside, just above the town, is the grave of the illustrious French leader, Gambetta.

BOUDOIR OF MARIE ANTOINETTE, TRIANON, VERSAILLES.—At one extremity of the Park of Versailles is the lovely little palace of Trianon, the favourite residence of poor Marie Antoinette. Her tastefully decorated boudoir is here given just as when occupied by her. This palace was originally given by Louis XV. to Madame du Barry, and the royal villa is still visible. But the special charm of Trianon lies in the garden around this royal villa abounding in shaded walks, beautiful trees, and artificial lake, and, above all, in the modest structures used by Marie Antoinette and the ladies of her Court when they came here to play the role of peasants. Weary of frivolity, the Queen would often turn gladly to the opposite extreme. Dressed in white muslin and a plain straw hat she would stroll along the paths, feeding chickens, chasing butterflies or joining in games of blind-man's buff and fox and geese. In one little building here, called her "Dairy," she and her friends would make butter on marble tables and laugh with glee at their moderate success. Another structure here is called the "Mill," where she insisted that her husband, Louis XVI., should play the part of miller, while she and her Court-ladies assumed the character and the dress of shepherdesses or simple peasant girls. It is pathetic to wander through these deserted though carefully kept grounds, and to think of the tragic fate of Marie Antoinette, who probably had no idea that Kings and Queens were created for any other object than to live in luxury. But in 1789 the clouds were rapidly gathering, and the storm was to burst upon "Little Trianon" with fearful violence. When the young Queen left this Park, and at the demand of the famished populace returned to Paris, she was destined to never see it again. It was her first step towards the guillotine.

WINDSOR CASTLE, ENGLAND.—An hour's ride by rail from London is this magnificent abode of royalty, the history of which dates from the time of William the Conqueror, eight hundred years ago. It is an intensely interesting place to visit, because so many different sovereigns have added something to its architecture and left to it still more imperishable souvenirs connected with their reigns. Such are the Gateway of Henry VIII., the Tower of Henry III., and St. George's Chapel, built by Edward IV. It is in this Chapel that take place at intervals the installations of the Knights of the Garter, that order which includes among its members so many Kings, Emperors, Princes and distinguished leaders of the race. The most conspicuous feature of old Windsor Castle is its immense "Round Tower," the view from which is beautiful and remarkably extensive. This tower is no less than 302 feet in circumference and 230 feet high. Whenever the flag floats over it, the public knows that the Queen is in the Castle, as is frequently the case. Like most mediæval strongholds, this royal abode is haunted by some gloomy memories. Captives have often languished here in misery. In the Round Tower, for example, the Prince who afterwards became James I. of Scotland was immured for eighteen years. In the Royal Vaults of Windsor are buried several of England's sovereigns, including Henry VIII. and his Queen, Lady Jane Seymour, the unfortunate Charles I., and the Princess Charlotte (only child of King George IV.), whose funeral monument is a magnificent work of art.

LIME STREET, LIVERPOOL, ENGLAND.—Nine-tenths of all the Americans who land in Liverpool stay there as little time as possible. Their memories of the place are chiefly those of a hurried struggle to get from the steamer to the railroad station, or from the railroad station to the steamer. The principal building, therefore, which they recollect in Liverpool is the one outlined in this illustration, namely, the London and Northwestern Hotel, upon the other side of which the trains of the London and Northwestern railroad start for London. As a matter of fact, however, Liverpool deserves more attention than is usually paid to it. It is the principal seaport of England and its second city. It contains more than 700,000 inhabitants. Its situation on the river Mersey is magnificent. Moreover, its famous docks, which flank the river for seven miles, have a total water area of 370 acres and 24 miles of quays! Nor are its architectural features of a low order. St. George's Hall, for example, directly opposite this hotel, must always command the admiration of even the most hasty traveller, for it is in the form of an immense Greek temple 600 feet long and 170 feet wide, adorned with Corinthian columns and many sculptures. Around this also are equestrian statues of Queen Victoria, the Prince Consort and the Earl of Beaconsfield. Some literary associations also make Liverpool interesting to intelligent tourists. It is the birthplace of the "Grand Old Man," Hon. W. E. Gladstone; and the house in which in 1809 he first saw the light (No. 62 Rodney street) is still visible. Here too in No. 32 Duke street was born the poetess, Mrs. Hemans; while Americans should not forget that in Liverpool from 1853 to 1857 the United States Consul was their gifted novelist, Nathaniel Hawthorne.

THE BANK OF ENGLAND, LONDON.—In the very heart of the city of London stands a low-browed, massive structure, streaked with soot and without even a window in its outer walls. It is the Bank of England. This absence of windows is supposed to give greater security to its valuable contents, the light within being received from interior courts and skylights. The structure looks therefore like a gigantic strong-box, covering four acres of territory! This establishment, though a national institution, is itself a private corporation. Its capital is about fifteen million pounds, and its bullion alone is supposed to be at least of the value of twenty-five million pounds sterling. Its affairs are managed by a governor, a deputy governor, twenty-four directors and nine hundred clerks. Below the surface of the ground there are more rooms in this structure than on the ground floor. One looks with almost a feeling of awe upon this building. Architecturally it has nothing to attract us, but we feel that it stands as a representative of the wealthiest and most influential empire on our globe. It has a lifeblood of its own which regulates the pulse of the financial world. Whatever is done within those massive walls will be felt in the Antipodes. One can hardly estimate the shock which the entire world would experience if public confidence in this institution were shaken. Almost the same thing can be said of it that was once affirmed of the Roman Colosseum. "While stands the Bank of England, England stands; When falls the Bank of England, England falls; When England falls—the world."

HOLYROOD PALACE, EDINBURGH, SCOTLAND.—At the other extremity of Edinburgh from that which holds its famous Castle is Holyrood Palace, the residence of Mary Queen of Scots. It is a gloomy building in appearance, whose cold gray walls seem to have little in harmony with the fair Queen, who once resided there. Her memory so completely haunts the place that, though this edifice has stood here for nearly 400 years, and though many Kings and Queens have lived within its walls, the apartments of Queen Mary are all that the traveller usually cares to see. Their contents are, however, slowly crumbling into dust, for the frail memorials of that unhappy lady have stood thus for 300 years. There are not many portraits of Mary here; but wherever they are hung they attract the attention of even the most careless tourist. Of all the thousands who have for centuries passed before them, probably not one has failed to pause and think with pity of the lovely woman whom they represent. Here also we may see the room in which Mary's secretary, the Italian Rizzio, was murdered by her jealous husband, Darnley; and certain stains are still pointed out as having been made by his blood. The ruined structure on the left of the palace is old Holyrood Chapel, where Rizzio was buried, and the imposing mountain rising in the background is called "Arthur's Seat."

EMPEROR'S PALACE, BERLIN.—In a prominent position on the Unter den Linden, and in close proximity to the Imperial Armoury and the magnificent statue of Frederick the Great, stands this residence of the late Emperor William I. The traveller is invariably surprised to find this edifice so unpretending. Compared with other palaces in Europe, it seems an insignificant abode for royalty, remarkable for neither decoration nor material; a plain, substantial house of stuccoed brick. A stranger might walk by and fancy it the home of some rich private individual, unless indeed the sentries at the door betrayed the presence of the sovereign. The corner windows of this building are those of the Emperor's study, and every day at noon, when the attendant regiment marched by to take its station at the guard house, at one of these windows could be seen the aged Kaiser and his great-grandchild, returning the salutations of the guard and populace. This custom the old Emperor maintained to the last days of his life; yet never did he thus present himself, save in full, soldier-like attire. In fact when dressed he never was without his uniform. True, in the privacy of his study, he would occasionally loosen and throw back his coat; but at the sound of fife or drum he always buttoned it again, and stood thus till the troops had passed. On being asked why he took such pains to fasten every button, he replied, "I wish to set a suitable example; for let me tell you, it is the *one* clasp left unbuttoned that is the ruin of an army."

UNTER DEN LINDEN, BERLIN.—From the great Brandenburg gate, which another illustration in this volume has revealed, extends through the heart of the city the most famous thoroughfare of the Prussian capital, the "Unter den Linden," or "Under the Lime Trees." The name is somewhat inappropriate at present, for there are few trees now in this busy street, and these are not in a very flourishing condition. Nevertheless, it is a highway of which the Berlinese are justly proud, straight as an arrow, more than a mile in length, and ornamented by many handsome buildings, such as the Arsenal and the palaces of Old Kaiser Wilhelm and the Crown Prince. Like most large German cities Berlin is admirably paved, and its streets are well kept and clean. Many of them are covered with asphalt, and in the early morning they are thoroughly washed, while a number of boys always follow up the watering-force with mops and sponges to remove the superfluous moisture. No one can visit Berlin to-day without feeling that it has arisen to be not only chief of Prussian cities, but the political centre of the German Empire. The increase in its population has been unparalleled among the world's great capitals. It is indeed to-day the brain and arm of that gigantic body known as United Germany; and it is Berlin (through her Rulers, Generals and Statesmen) which has in the last few decades transformed the Germany of poetry, legend and romantic ruins into the greatest military power upon the earth—the Germany of blood and iron, of cannon and of conquest—of Bismarck and Von Moltke.

THE QUAYS OF ANTWERP, BELGIUM.—The name Antwerp is said to be derived from the Flemish words meaning "On the Wharf;" and that indeed is the place where Antwerp's prosperity can be best estimated. It is a place of wonderful activity, and these its splendid quays—built by Napoleon I. when Antwerp formed a part of his colossal empire—are crowded now with ships and steamers. Yet busy as it is to-day, it gives us but a *hint* of what its commerce was 300 years ago! Then thousands of vessels floated in the river, and more than 500 were arriving and departing every day. Merchants came hither from all parts of Europe, and, in addition to her own commercial houses, more than 1,000 foreign firms contended here in friendly rivalry. Antwerp, however, has had much to contend with since that time. Again and again this region has been the "cock-pit of Europe," and for years Antwerp's wealth and prosperity declined. But now she is rapidly recovering from her disasters. Give her but half a century more of peace under as good a government as that of her liberal King Leopold, and she will take long strides to re-assume the place which she once occupied, that of the leading maritime city of the world.

THE ROYAL PALACE, BRUSSELS, BELGIUM.—Close by the pretty park of Brussels stands this residence of Belgium's royal family. Its exterior is not very handsome, but it **is** furnished with great elegance. Leopold II. is much respected and beloved by his subjects. He is an intelligent, refined and accomplished gentleman and a wise sovereign. It would **be** difficult to find in Europe a nation better governed, a constitution more implicitly obeyed, a King more liberal and progressive, and a people happier and more prosperous than in Belgium. One might select worse places for a European residence than this bright capital of the Belgians. Why English and Americans who wish to live abroad, sometimes to study French, should almost always go to Paris, where the great foreign colony and the incessant whirl of gaiety make study almost an impossibility, is not quite easy to explain. The French of Brussels **is** remarkable for its purity, and certainly the life there is much more agreeable than in the smaller towns of France, like Tours, Bordeaux and Orleans, so much frequented by American and English families. The expense of living here is also moderate, and the Belgians themselves are an extremely courteous and attractive people.

THUN AND THE BERNESE ALPS, SWITZERLAND.—In the heart of Switzerland are two lovely bodies of water, Lake Thun and Lake Brienze. Between these lakes, as its name denotes, is *Interlaken*, one of the most delightful places of sojourn in the whole circuit of the Alps. Which of the lakes which lie to either side of it is the more beautiful is hard to say. The one presented here is possibly the more attractive. At all events the steamboat journey of ten miles over its deep blue surface affords a series of enchanting views, and finally brings one to this picturesque town of Thun itself, situated just where the River Aar emerges from the lake, and for a moment slackens here its pace, as if reluctant to depart; conscious perhaps that now it is about to leave the Alpine region of its birth, and turning towards the level countries and the sea, become apprenticed to the *Rhine*, and with that mightier master lead a life of labour and care. All the great world of travel passes through Thun and over its mountain-bordered lake to Interlaken almost of necessity. No other spot in Switzerland is quite so central for excursions; none is more easy of approach. From 60,000 to 80,000 people come to this region every summer. The glorious Bernese Alps are just beyond, conspicuous among which is the queenly Jungfrau, which forms a dazzling object of attraction, a radiant centre-piece of ice and snow nearly 14,000 feet in height.

MAXIMILIAN PLATZ, VIENNA.—This handsome square is only one of the many features of Vienna which remind us of Paris. No other European capitals are so alike in architecture, character and customs. Both are pre-eminently beautiful and brilliant, and both have points in history which possess a strong resemblance. Both, for example, were originally Roman settlements. In each a Cæsar has resided. The Emperor Julian living in the one; Marcus Aurelius dying in the other. In modern times the most ill-fated of French Queens was the unhappy daughter of Maria Theresa, Marie Antoinette; while from Vienna also comes Napoleon's second wife, whose son, born heir to an inheritance on which the boldest gazed with bated breath, died in obscurity within the palace of an Austrian Emperor. On one side of this square we see the exquisitely sculptured spires of a Gothic church, erected to commemorate the present Emperor's escape from assassination. For notwithstanding his great popularity, a miscreant was found some years ago desirous of killing him. This he attempted to accomplish by aiming at his throat with a dagger; the gilt upon the Emperor's military collar, however, turned the point of the weapon, and his life was saved. As for the church, it is so beautiful as to make one almost glad that the assassination was attempted! There is no part of it that does not call for admiration; but especially delicate and graceful are these pointed towers embellished with a multitude of statues and arising to the lofty height of 345 feet. Through that open fret-work the stars are visible at night, as through the interlacing branches of the trees.

THE LOGGIA, FLORENCE.—Close by the grand Palazzo Vecchio and on another side of the Square of the Senate is a marble portico of vast proportions. It is the celebrated Loggia or Portico of the Lancers, so called from the Dukes' spearmen formerly stationed here beside the Palace. How simple yet beautiful is this arcade of lofty arches curving in perfect symmetry! For more than five eventful centuries it has remained here thus, delighting every visitor to Florence from the most casual observer to the skilled architect. When Lorenzo di Medici begged Michael Angelo to plan for him another splendid ornament for this Piazza, the sculptor answered: "Carry that Loggia entirely around it. Nothing finer can possibly be invented." The Prince, however, shrank from the expense of the undertaking. No lancers are stationed here to-day. For centuries it has had a noble use, since it now forms a most imposing canopy of shelter for rare works of art, which thus in Florence literally *overflow* from her great sculpture galleries into the streets themselves! Here for example is the masterpiece in bronze of Benvenuto Cellini, his celebrated "Perseus holding up the head of the monster Medusa," and near that is the marble group by John of Bologna, entitled the "Rape of the Sabines." This Loggia therefore displays an exhibition of sculpture such as we never see on the American side of the Atlantic, exposed freely and continually to the admiration and inspection of every passer-by.

GRAND CANAL, VENICE.—Few experiences in life are more enjoyable than the traveller's first sail on the canals of Venice, that city which perhaps more than any other has towered up in the horizon of our imagination since childhood, and whose very name, so soon as it is pronounced, serves as a spell to stimulate our fancy and enthusiasm. The Grand Canal is the princely avenue of Venice. It winds through the city in a graceful curve, bordered for miles on either side by marble palaces and churches, some of which, though crumbling to decay, still attest the magnificence of by-gone days. One can hardly imagine anything more unreal yet beautiful, more like a vision in some happy dream, than these grand stately buildings of the past glittering in the moonlight and floating thus in splendour on the sea. Late though the hour be, in some of these palaces lights are sure to be gleaming through the casement; and, if we bid our gondolier halt a moment beneath the magic lights and shadows of their balconies, we may often hear within the tinkling sound of the guitar, or the voice of some unseen musician. From time to time our boatman will impart to some of these an added interest by pausing in his measured stroke to whisper in his soft Venetian dialect some well-known name, some story or some tragic memory which haunt their massive walls. Thus we have pointed out to us the palace in which the poet Byron lived; the house of the Doge Dandolo, Conqueror of Constantinople, and the palace of Marino Faliero, decapitated for his crimes.

STATUE OF LIBERTY, NEW YORK HARBOUR.—Standing out in sublime proportions against the sun-set sky, the colossal statue of Liberty seems one of the most impressive works of man which can be found upon this continent. It is indeed gigantic, having a height of 151 feet! Yet despite its enormous size, it is so perfectly proportioned that one beholds it with complete satisfaction. This noble work of the French sculptor, Bartholdi, is fortunate in its position, which gives to it an independent, queenly and even threatening aspect. It stands on Bedloe's Island, about two miles from the city. It is made of repoussé copper, and represents a female figure crowned with a diadem. One arm presses a tablet closely to her breast; the other holds aloft a blazing torch. Its great height is intensified by the huge granite pedestal which is itself 155 feet high. A stairway leads to the head of the statue, in which several people can be easily accommodated at one time. At night this colossal figure seems even more imposing than by day. Whoever has sailed near it at such a time will recollect the awe-inspiring effect produced by that Titanic figure rising through the gloom, its vast dimensions magnified by a sombre background, while the uplifted torch glitters with electricity, as a star flashes when we view it through a telescope. A few statistics may well be mentioned here. This statue can be seen distinctly at a distance of four or five miles. Its total height above low water mark is 306 feet. The fore-finger of its right hand is seven feet long, and over four feet in circumference at the second joint. It weighs over twenty-five tons, and cost more than a million francs (£40,000), which was paid for by popular subscriptions in France.

THE LOUVRE, PARIS.—This splendid edifice, standing in the very heart of Paris, appeals to us in at least three ways. Its architecture is of the highest excellence and satisfies the eye from every point; its history is also full of interest; and finally, as a noble Treasure-house of Art, it becomes one of the most important buildings in the world. The foundation of the Louvre is of great antiquity, dating from the year 1200. It was used as a royal residence down to the time of Louis XIV., who removed the Court to the magnificent Palace of Versailles. Here was solemnized in 1572 the marriage between Henry IV., "the gallant Henry of Navarre," and the fair Margaret of Valois; and five days later, on the night of the 24th of August, the signal was here given for the massacre of the Huguenots on the eve of "St. Bartholomew." The window is shown where Charles IX. fired that night on the crowd of fugitives. The two Napoleons greatly enlarged and embellished the Louvre, and formed the two long arms which finally united it with the Palace of the Tuilleries. The Louvre collections of antiquities, gems, statuary and paintings, are of incalculable value, yet are opened freely to the public. Volumes are required merely to briefly catalogue the treasures here contained, the possession of which gives to Paris a transcendent importance for all students and lovers of art. Incredible as it would seem, in 1871 the Communists tried to destroy this entire building with its priceless contents. It was a piece of vandalism which disgraces the nineteenth century. The Imperial Library of 90,000 volumes was thus destroyed, but happily the government troops arrived in time to prevent further losses.

TRAFALGAR SQUARE, LONDON.—This handsome square is so centrally located that it may be said to form the nucleus or heart of London. Around it are the National Gallery of Paintings, the celebrated St. Martin's Church, and such hotels as "Morley's" and the "Metropole," while in the centre rises a majestic column known as the Nelson monument, surmounted at a height of 154 feet by a statue of the immortal hero who died victorious at Trafalgar in 1805. Upon the pedestal are inscribed Nelson's well-known words, "England expects that every man will do his duty." Flanking this granite monument are the four colossal lions of Sir Edwin Landseer, which are not only magnificent specimens of art, but are thoroughly in keeping with the majestic severity of the shaft which they adorn as well as with the leonine character of the great admiral beneath whose statue they thus crouch submissively. This London Square has little of the charm and beauty of the Place de la Concorde in Paris, yet it is thoroughly characteristic of the city in which it stands. The qualities which attract us in London are quite different from those which please us on the other side of the channel; but when one has at last become accustomed to its smoky atmosphere, its melancholy fogs and sombre architecture, there is so much in London to appeal to the students of history, art, archæology, science and human nature (to say nothing of the interest awakened in us by associations with the English novelists and poets, who have often made this great metropolis their theme), that one can agree with Dr. Johnson when he said, "The happiness of London cannot be conceived except by those who have beheld it."

CUSTOM HOUSE, DUBLIN, IRELAND.—Dublin has several noble edifices, among which is its Custom House, opened in 1791, and erected at a cost of about £400,000. Standing on the north side of the river Liffey, which flows directly through the city, it is seen on three sides to admirable advantage. From the centre rises a dome 125 feet high and surmounted by a statue symbolical of an invariable characteristic of the Irish, HOPE. Notwithstanding this handsome structure, Dublin has not so much business activity as we should expect to find in so large and important a city, and Belfast is said to transact a larger general trade. The docks in the river have been improved, the river itself has been deepened, and new wharves have been constructed, but the custom dues have for many years remained almost stationary. Dublin produces little for exportation now save whiskey and porter. It has now but few manufactures and these are of trifling value. The public buildings of Dublin which rival this Custom House in elegance of architecture, are the Bank of Ireland (formerly the House of Parliament), St. Patrick's Cathedral, and above all, Trinity College, which is an honour not only to Ireland, but to Great Britain. Like every other great city, Dublin has its poor quarters, and an excursion through its slums is as interesting as the tours through the East End of London which were so fashionable a few years ago. But even there the happy buoyant disposition of the people of the Emerald Isle is conspicuous, and the poverty is nowhere accompanied by the terrible and obvious misery that alone can account for the pinched faces and irrevocable despair that are so painfully apparent in some districts of the capital of the empire.

PRINCE BISMARCK'S FORMER OFFICIAL RESIDENCE, BERLIN.—The plain unostentatious house which will always be associated with the memory of the great Chancellor of the German Empire has a strange interest for the tourist. When the Prince was in residence it was always possible to find a crowd of persons waiting before it, in the hope of catching a glimpse of him; for, in spite of the fact that Bismarck is known as "the man of blood and iron," his personality has always been intensely popular. Indeed, the devotion of the people to Bismarck is second only to their devotion to their Kaiser, and the reconciliation which followed the temporary estrangement between the young Emperor and the aged soldier was not only a touching historic incident, but an opportunity, eagerly embraced, for the people of the Empire to express at once their loyalty to the throne and their affection to one of the greatest of the founders of a united Germany. The memory of Bismarck will live not only as that of the relentless soldier, but as that of the statesman and the man, full of years and honour, living his quiet country life with his home ties and his big dogs—a man loved as well as feared. The Prince's old home in Berlin is chiefly interesting for his sake, and its interest is as great as that of any royal palace in Europe.

DUTCH WINDMILLS, HOLLAND.—Two characteristic features of Holland constantly present themselves, canals and windmills. The latter really seem innumerable. The country often appears to be alive with these revolving monsters, which, when in motion, look like giants turning hand-screws on the horizon, and when at rest resemble light-houses above the sea. But "rest" with them is rare! They are employed for almost every kind of manufacture. They grind corn, they saw wood, they cut tobacco into snuff, they pulverize rocks, and (most important of all) they pump out from the marshes into the canals the water which would otherwise submerge the entire land. The largest ones will, it is claimed, in a fair wind, lift 10,000 gallons of water per minute to the height of four feet! One can but admire the wisdom of the persevering Hollanders, who have thus yoked the inconstant wind and forced it not alone to work for them, but also to contend with their great enemy, Water! It is a realization of the rough but wholesome words of Emerson, when he says: "Borrow the strength of the elements. Hitch your wagon to a star, and see the chores done by the gods themselves." A Hollander's wealth is often estimated, not by his bonds or mortgages, but by his windmills. "How rich is such a man?" you may ask. "Oh, he is worth ten or twelve windmills," is the reply!

THE BAY OF NAPLES, ITALY.—It is a never-to-be-forgotten moment when one looks for the first time on this unrivalled bay, which holds within its glorious curve Pompeii and Sorrento, forever guarded by the giant form of fire-scathed Vesuvius. Incomparably fair is the environment of Naples; its winding shores, its sparkling bay, its bold cliffs ravaged by the sea, its threatening lava cone and buried city of Pompeii, all these combine to render it a veritable Mecca for lovers of the beautiful. To drive along the northern shore of this Neapolitan Bay is to explore the hallowed ground of classical Italy. At every turn the souvenirs of ancient times seem waiting to receive us, clad in the pleasing garb of legend or tradition, while in every breath that blows upon us from this classic sea, we hear a murmur of ancient yet familiar names. For, once these slopes were covered with the splendid villas of distinguished Romans; and therefore history and fable blend now their dark and golden threads to weave a net-work of enchantment round the place. Thus it is well known that Virgil had a villa on this shore, in which he lived for years, composing some of his finest works; and when he died, the Emperor caused his friend's last wish to be fulfilled, and had his body brought here for interment, beside the same unchanging sea and on the very slope were he had written his immortal poems.

THE PIAZZETTA, VENICE.—Extending at right angles to the Piazza of San Marco, which is the great square of Venice and the Forum of Venetian life and history, is this smaller esplanade known by the pretty diminutive, "Piazzetta." At one extremity of it glitter the blue waters of the Grand Canal, fringed with a row of gondolas ("dusky spirits of the canal"), which float there in the sunshine, tempting the tourist to glide out on a fascinating voyage of exploration in this most poetic and romantic of cities. Two noble granite columns cut their outlines here against the eastern sky. They were brought hither from one of the Greek Islands as trophies of Venetian conquest in 1127. There were originally three of these colossal shafts, but one fell into the sea as it was being landed, and could not be recovered. One of the two erected here is surmounted by the characteristic symbol of Venice, the winged Lion of St. Mark ; the other by a statue of St. Theodore, who was the patron saint of the Republic before St. Mark's body was brought hither from Egypt in 827. The Doge of Venice having promised to fulfil "any fair request" made by the man who should safely land and erect these columns here, the successful architect demanded that gambling, elsewhere prohibited, should be permitted between them. The promise was faithfully kept ; but to render it of no practical use, it was ordered that all public executions should take place there. This made the spot so "unlucky" in the eyes of gamesters that they deserted it voluntarily. On the left of this Piazza is the magnificent Palace of the Doges, elsewhere described.

PALERMO AND MONTE PELLEGRINO, PALERMO, SICILY.—The island of Sicily is a portion of our earth which has entranced the hearts of all men from the time of Homer to our own. Fortunately more travellers now go thither every year, for the government of Italy has rendered travelling there secure, and railroads have removed many former hardships. A city in Sicily whose situation is almost unrivalled in the world for beauty is Palermo. For centuries this has been named *La Felice*, or the "Happy One." Nor is this strange; for the hill-girt plain on which it lies is still called, both from its fertility and curving form, La Conca d'Oro, or the "Shell of Gold." "As fruitful as Palermo!" No land needs higher praise than this. For its surrounding valley is one vast grove of lemons and of oranges which every year sends forth its golden harvest over half the world. At one extremity of Palermo is a most picturesque object, namely, the enormous Rock of Monte Pellegrino, which rises to a height of 2,000 feet, like a monster of the sea to shield the city from the Northern winds. "The Mt. of Pilgrims" is the meaning of its musical title, and countless are the pilgrims who resort thither in a single year. Many centuries ago a fair Sicilian maiden named Rosalia fled to that gloomy mountain to live apart from the world in prayer and meditation. This was strange enough, but stranger still is the tradition that, when the plague was raging here in 1664, a lucky priest discovered there in a cave the body of Rosalia perfectly preserved, although she had been dead five hundred years! When this was brought into the city, the effect was wonderful, for the plague is said to have disappeared at once, and Santa Rosalia has ever since been the patron saint of Palermo, and her name has been given to the Cathedral itself.

PUERTA DEL SOL, MADRID, SPAIN.—This "Portal of the Sun" was formerly the eastern Gateway of Madrid, and hence the first to be greeted by the dawn, but now it marks the centre of the capital. Although not beautiful, it is nevertheless justly famous, for it is the nucleus of the city's life, the *heart* of Madrid, throbbing with tireless activity. Through this the restless life-blood of the town is every moment flowing. Most of the lower stories of its houses and hotels are cafés, from which at night music and light stream forth, amid a clatter of glasses, a babbling of tongues and the cries of waiters, as though this Spanish capital had banished sleep forever. Sun-burnt peasants and ragged beggars are always idling about in this Puerta, gaining fresh coats of tan by steeping themselves in the sun. One can always perceive here Spanish priests, dressed in their great three-cornered hats and long black robes, amid a mass of gaily-decorated mules with tinkling bells, bull fighters in their gorgeous costumes, musicians with guitars, and proud Castilians wrapped in their deftly-folded cloaks and wearing on their heads those huge sombreros which strikingly resemble gigantic chocolate creams. If you are in the mood for it, this whirl of life is thoroughly amusing. If not, it renders you more sad than would the desert. For in that motley throng there is not one who knows your name, or cares for your existence. One may find cause for sadness, therefore, even in this brilliant Gateway of the Sun.

OPORTO, PORTUGAL.—Oporto was once the capital of Portugal, and is now its second city, yielding only to Lisbon in importance. Even now more traffic is carried on here than at the capital itself. It is beautifully located on high bluffs along the River Douro, which here rolls downward like a flood of silver to the sea five miles away. The approach to it is imposing. For miles on either side are terraced vineyards glistening in the sun, reminding one of the borders of the Rhine, for this too is a favourite haunt of Bacchus, and Oporto is the emporium of the rich "Port" wine to which the city gives its name. Although its streets are very steep, it is a clean and attractive place, and foreigners residing here speak in high terms of its agreeable qualities. Many English firms are established in Oporto, and their immense store-houses in which the port wine is kept extend for a considerable distance along the quays. Spanning the Douro, and looking in the distance like a thread of gossamer, is a light and elegant suspension bridge connecting Oporto with a suburb on the opposite bank. Superbly situated cities, like Lisbon and Oporto, remind us of the time when gallant fleets sailed out from them upon their paths of conquest and discovery, in those days of Portuguese glory, when the King of France wrote in jealousy to the sovereign of Portugal these words: "Since you and the King of Spain have undertaken to divide the world between you, will you kindly show to me a copy of the will of our Father Adam, which makes you two the heirs of all his property!"

WINTER PALACE, ST. PETERSBURG, RUSSIA.—This magnificent abode of the Czar is a most imposing structure extending on one side for a long distance beside the river Neva, and on the other facing an enormous square adorned with a lofty monolithic shaft, known as the Alexander Column.   The walls of this Palace have the great defect of being covered with stucco, and hence in the springtime, when St. Petersburg is emerging from the winter's frosts, this Imperial residence often presents a dilapidated appearance.   Nevertheless, its vast size and admirable situation make it exceedingly impressive, and many of its halls and rooms are furnished with great magnificence.   It was in this palace that the late Czar, Alexander II., narrowly escaped death by the blowing up of the Imperial dining-room, just before he entered it ; and here it was, in less than a year after that attempt, that he expired, having been brought hither from the neighbouring street in which the bombs of Nihilists had horribly mangled his body.   No one can look upon this Winter Palace, and then turn to survey the mighty city around it, without admiring the indomitable will and courage of Peter the Great, who chose this marshy bank of the Neva for his capital, and built it here in spite of all the obstacles which man and Nature placed in his path.   Yes, when we look upon the subjugated river Neva, sweeping along in majesty, yet curbed by twenty miles of granite quays ; and when we admire St. Petersburg's imposing palaces, its granite monoliths, its churches built of marble, bronze and gold, and its broad avenues where hundreds can march abreast, we realize that it is to Peter the Great that all this is justly attributable, and we feel that it is most appropriate that this great capital should bear the name of its creator.

THE PARTHENON, ATHENS.—The glory of Athens was the hill called the Acropolis, which rose four hundred feet above the town, covered with wonderful temples and statues; and the especial glory of the Acropolis was the Parthenon. To this ascended from the city a marble stairway sixty-two feet in breadth, entirely composed of marble and adorned with statues, the mutilated remains of which we revere to-day in the art galleries of Europe. The Parthenon itself is a matchless edifice even in its ruin. No photographic view can do it justice, for its marble columns are somewhat weather-stained and look in the illustration as if they were dingy and dark like the soot-covered buildings of London. But this is not so. The discolorations are so *light* as to be hardly blemishes; while the general appearance of the building is one of snowy whiteness. This temple stood here comparatively unchanged in its unrivalled beauty, until two centuries ago. But in 1670, during a bombardment of the city, a shell exploded in this shrine, where had been rashly stored a quantity of powder, and instantly with one wild roar, as though nature itself were shrieking at the sacrilege, the Parthenon was ruined! Columns on either side were blown to atoms, severing the front of the temple from the rear, and covering the whole plateau with marble fragments—mute witnesses of countless forms of beauty, forever lost to us. Happily, however, enough of this Parthenon remains to show the literal *perfection* of its masonry, with curves so delicate as to be hardly perceptible to the eye, yet true to the 1-100th part of an inch, and showing alike the splendid genius of the architect and the wonderful skill of the workmen.

CAPE SPARTEL, TANGIER, AFRICA.—The distance from Gibraltar to Tangier in Morocco is about seventy miles. This Strait of Gibraltar, like the channel between France and England, is almost always rough; but the scenery along the two confronting coasts of Europe and Africa is most imposing. Snow-covered mountains rise in Africa as well as in Spain. At one point near Tangier a promontory, called Cape Spartel, advances boldly into the waves. Upon its summit glitters in the sun a white-walled lighthouse and tower of observation. From this the view of the ocean is magnificent. Tangier itself is a most melancholy proof of the degeneracy of that cultivated race which built the Alhambra at Granada and ruled in Spain for seven centuries. Its streets are merely narrow, dirty alleys. There are few, if any, wheeled vehicles there. Apparently the sparkling channel which rolls here between Spain and Morocco proves an insurmountable barrier to the advent of European civilization. Yet in the Governor's Palace in Tangier there are several rusty keys, said to have once unlocked the doors of Moorish houses in Granada, and therefore held by the descendants of the exiles of four hundred years ago as priceless souvenirs of their once glorious past. A few miles from the city on a high plateau are the residences of the American Minister, various foreign Consuls and a few wealthy European merchants. The view from these dwellings resembles this from Cape Spartel, and is not only beautiful, but thronged with those historic memories which make the classic Mediterranean the most interesting sheet of water on the globe.

BETHLEHEM, PALESTINE.—In looking at any city in the Holy Land one always sees a multitude of flat-roofed houses made of stone cement or sun-dried bricks. Whatever beauty such towns possess is to be found in their natural surroundings, not in the structures themselves. Bethlehem is situated in a fertile region which gave to the place its name; for Bethlehem in Hebrew signifies "the place of food." Every reader of these lines of course knows the prominent part which this town has played in Jewish history. It was the scene of the beautiful story of Ruth, and as the residence of the family of David it was especially revered by Hebrew prophets and poets. During the Christian era it has been the resort of millions of pilgrims who have come century after century in undiminished numbers to worship at the shrine of Christ's nativity. The church erected over the reputed birthplace of Jesus is of enormous size and is owned by Greeks, Latins and Armenians. For more than 1,500 years at least the site has never changed. Here on Christmas day, 1101, the Crusader Baldwin was crowned King of Jerusalem. The tomb of Saint Jerome is also shown at Bethlehem, and it is an undoubted fact that that illustrious father of the Church resided here for many years, dying A. D. 420. Here he learned Hebrew of the Jews, and translated the whole Bible from the original into Latin. Various chapels are erected here to commemorate the Adoration of the Magi, the Slaughter of the Innocents, and most of the events connected with the birth of Christ.

BUNKER HILL MONUMENT, NEAR BOSTON, MASS.—The suburb of Boston, known as Charlestown, is made conspicuous in history as well as in the landscape by a tall granite shaft, which, plain, severe and substantial as the Puritans themselves, looks down upon the surrounding country. It stands upon the summit of the little hill, where on the night of the 16th of June, 1775, a small redoubt was erected by the American patriots to resist the British. The real name of this eminence was "Breed's Hill," but *Bunker Hill* seems to have been the general term for the locality, and that title has been ever since associated with the battle which took place on the 17th of June. On the fiftieth anniversary of this conflict, in 1825, the Marquis of La Fayette laid with his own hands the corner-stone of this granite monument, which is thirty feet square at its base and 221 feet high. A spiral flight of 295 steps leads to the summit, whence a magnificent view is obtained of Boston, its harbour and its suburbs. This shaft was dedicated on the 17th of June, 1843, in the presence of President Tyler and all the members of his Cabinet. It was on that occasion that the orator of Massachusetts, Daniel Webster, pronounced the dedicatory oration, which is usually considered the most eloquent and impressive speech that he ever delivered. In a house near the monument is a statue of General Warren, who was killed here in the battle. This circumstance recalls to all the well-known story of the proud citizen of Boston who was explaining this locality to a country visitor. "This is the spot," he said, "where Warren fell." Looking up at the monument and measuring its height, the countryman replied, "Gracious! No wonder that it killed him!"

BEACH AT ATLANTIC CITY, NEW JERSEY.—One of the most attractive and popular ocean-resorts along the eastern coast of the United States is Atlantic City, in New Jersey. To a certain extent all fashionable sea-side places resemble each other. A multitude of hotels with broad piazzas, innumerable cottages in their vicinity, wicker chairs for invalids, fine music, dancing, flirtation, thousands of promenaders on the extensive piers, and above all the gay, hilarious, scantily-dressed bathers in the surf—all these are features to be found at almost every watering-place, both in the Old World and the New. 'Tis true the language in which the menus are printed or in which love is made beside the sea may differ widely in these various lands, but the deep murmur of the restless ocean is the same, whether it beats itself against the rocks at Biarritz, breaks in reverberation on the dunes of Holland, or dies in softer cadence on the sandy beach of our Atlantic City; just as the human heart with all its loves, hopes, happiness, anxiety and despair is everywhere fundamentally the same, although the audible expressions of its deep emotions will vary as nativity or education may demand. The view of the Atlantic from this place is wonderfully fine! The water is by no means so cold as on the shores of New England; the bathing facilities are almost unexcelled; and its nearness to Philadelphia, Trenton, Wilmington and other eastern cities makes it a favourite place for thousands of people, wearied by the stifling heat of pavements and brick walls, to fly for at least the respite of a Saturday and Sunday by the waves.

THE GUTENBERG MONUMENT, FRANKFORT.—It commemorates first and foremost John Gutenberg, but with him are associated his contemporaries, Fust and Schoeffer. Below this group an ornamental frieze presents a series of medallions of subsequent printers. Below these again are statues representing the cities of Mainz (Gutenberg's birthplace), Strasburg, Venice and Frankfort, in all of which this invention made rapid progress. On the corners are allegorical figures portraying Theology, Poetry, Science and Industry. To Gutenberg really belongs the glory of having invented movable types for printing. Up to that time it had been necessary to use engraved plates of wood or metal. Fust was a goldsmith who advanced money to Gutenberg to help on his experiment, taking, however, as security, a mortgage on all the printing materials. Gutenberg was at first unsuccessful as far as pecuniary results were concerned, and Fust, who had advanced more money, foreclosed the mortgage, seized the materials and took them to Mainz. There he, with his son-in-law Schoeffer, carried on the work. Several important books had already been printed by Gutenberg in 1455, among which was a large folio Latin Bible. Fust and Schoeffer together printed in Mainz till 1462. The art was then fairly established and was destined to revolutionize the world. Poor Gutenberg died in 1468, childless, almost friendless, and in want. But among the heroes of the Rhineland and the benefactors of the race, his name stands out in characters which will forever command the attention of posterity.

12

THE MADONNA DI SAN SISTO, DRESDEN GALLERY.—Among the treasures of the picture gallery at Dresden the most highly valued is the Sistine Madonna painted by Raphael as an altar-piece in the cloister of San Sisto, in Piacenza, Italy. In 1753 it was purchased by the King of Saxony, for about ten thousand pounds, and was removed to Dresden, where it still remains. Green curtains drawn aside reveal the wondrous scene. Relieved against a background of cherubs' heads, which gradually fade away into celestial radiance, stands forth enthroned upon the clouds the Virgin with the Divine Child in her arms. On one side the venerable Pope Sixtus gazes upward in reverence, and on the other is revealed Santa Barbara, whose eyes are cast downward, as if unable or unworthy to contemplate this vision of Divinity and exalted Humanity. In the foreground are the two well-known and exquisitely beautiful Cherubs, apparently too absorbed in their own happy innocence to be aware of the transcendent meaning of the scene of which it is their privilege to form a part. The whole appearance of the Virgin is one of triumph, inspiring awe, as well as admiration; while the look in the eyes of the youthful Jesus is almost superhuman, as though they were gazing down the vista of the coming years and could already see within that sad perspective the Crown of Thorns, the Garden of Gethsemane and the three Crosses on the hill of Calvary.

THE PALAZZO VECCHIO, FLORENCE.—One of the first objects which the traveller beholds as he approaches Florence, and certainly one of the first to which he pays a visit, is this massive structure called the Palazzo Vecchio, or Old Palace. This was built in the year 1298, and served as the Senate House of Florence during the Republic, and later still as the official residence of the Medici, that famous family which gave eight Dukes to Tuscany, two Queens to France, and four Popes to the Vatican. What an amount of history is centred in that gloomy edifice, and *cruel* history at that! That same imposing tower, 330 feet in height, and these same palace walls were in 1498 reddened by the glare of Savonarola's burning form, and echoed to the curses of that fickle multitude which had so often hung upon his words, yet then thronged every window, roof and balcony to witness his death agony. Yet when the reaction came, this building also saw for centuries, upon the anniversary of that dreadful day, the pavement of this Square covered with violets, in memory of the good which Savonarola had achieved, and repentance for his cruel death. The tower of this Palazzo Vecchio commands a magnificent view, and one may see within it the prison of Savonarola.

BORGUND CHURCH, NORWAY.—As the tourist in Norway is driving through the grand mountain scenery which is spread broadcast along the Norwegian coast and at the inner extremities of its wonderful fjords, there suddenly appears before him an extraordinary building, on which he gazes with astonishment. It seems more appropriate to China than to Norway, and looks completely out of place in this wild, desolate ravine. It is the famous Borgund Church, a place of early Christian worship, erected here about 800 years ago. With the exception of one other similar structure, it is the oldest building in all Norway. It is so small that one could almost fancy it a sanctuary for dwarfs. Around the base is a kind of cloister, from which the dim interior receives its only light. Within is one small room about thirty-nine feet long, containing now no furniture except a rough-hewn wooden altar. As for its various pinnacles and turrets, nothing could be more weirdly picturesque ; for they are surmounted now by crosses, now by dragons' heads, and the colour of the entire edifice is almost black, partly from the coats of pitch with which it has been painted for protection. Near by is another curious structure, now crumbling into ruin, which served as a belfry to the church itself.

THE COLUMN OF JULY, PARIS.—At one extremity of the principal Boulevards of Paris rises this imposing monument in bronze. It was erected in honour of the patriots who fell in the revolution of July, 1830, but the place on which it stands recalls even more stirring associations than those of the "July" struggle for liberty. For this enclosure is the Place de la Bastille, the site of that terrible State Prison of old France, the very name of which, "The Bastille," is synonymous with cruelty and infamous injustice. The first great act of the maddened populace in 1789 (which also took place in the month of July) was the destruction of this stronghold of tyranny. Some of the stones of the Bastille were used in the construction of one of the bridges crossing the Seine. They are now, therefore, daily trampled under foot by thousands of liberated Frenchmen. It is appropriate that this "July Column", should have upon its summit, 154 feet above the square, a statue of liberty, holding in one hand a torch and in the other a broken chain. In 1871 the Communists filled the vaults beneath this monument with gunpowder, intending to blow up the column and ruin the entire neighbourhood. Happily the attempt was frustrated, and the historic shaft still stands unharmed.

LAST DAYS OF NAPOLEON AT ST. HELENA (By Vela), VERSAILLES.—It is not merely the dying Napoleon whom we here behold—it is the Exile, the dethroned Emperor, the heart-broken Captive, forgotten by those whom he had raised from the dust and made illustrious, abandoned by his Austrian wife, and deprived of any communication with his idolized child. The grand Napoleonic head is here, which always shows so admirably in marble. The forehead is the same as that which wore the coronet of France and the iron crown of Charlemagne, but his temples are sunken and his cavernous eyes seem gazing down the vista of the years of captivity to the time when he was master of Europe and made or unmade kings at will. In his lap is the outspread map of Europe, upon which rests his nerveless hand. That hand once carved out kingdoms there. It is now powerless to trace his name! Surely this statue (true to life and history) tells us that if Napoleon greatly sinned, he suffered correspondingly. To rise from the position of an obscure lieutenant of artillery to be the conqueror of half of Europe and sovereign of France and Italy; to place his family on the thrones of Holland, Spain, Naples and Westphalia, to equal Cæsar in his victories, to wed a daughter of the Austrian Emperor, to plan to have his son succeed him in his glorious dynasty, and then to lose it all and linger on, chained like Prometheus to a barren rock, his heart continually gnawed by the implacable vulture of Regret—what tragedy has the world beheld to equal it? Better to fall like the first Cæsar, 'neath the daggers of conspirators, than die by inches on a seagirt cliff, as did the Cæsar of the Nineteenth Century.

TOMB OF NAPOLEON, PARIS.—Beneath the gilded dome of the Invalides is one of the most impressive sights on earth. In a vast marble-lined apartment the visitor leans over a circular marble railing and looks on a crypt twenty feet deep and thirty-six feet in diameter. There on a pavement of mosaic in the form of a star around which are inscribed the names of Bonaparte's most brilliant victories (Rivoli, Austerlitz, Marengo, Wagram, The Pyramids, Moscow, etc.), rises a grand sarcophagus of porphyry, a single block of stone brought hither from Finland, and weighing sixty-seven tons. It is the tomb of Napoleon. Around this crypt are twelve colossal statues of Victory, and several groups of battle-flags captured in the Napoleonic wars. A coloured light from stained glass windows in the roof invests this solemn circle of the dead with an ineffable solemnity. The entrance of the crypt is flanked by two sarcophagi, the burial places of the Emperor's friends, Duroc and Bertrand, one of whom died in battle for his adored chieftain, while the other followed Napoleon to St. Helena and shared his pitiable captivity until by Death the imperial captive was at last set free. Above the entrance to the crypt are these words from Napoleon's will dictated at St. Helena: "I desire that my ashes may repose on the banks of the Seine, among that French people I so dearly loved." His wish has been fulfilled. No more magnificent sepulchre exists on earth than that which shelters here the ashes of the great Napoleon.

CHURCH OF ST. BASIL, MOSCOW, RUSSIA.—St. Basil's church is one of the most extraordinary buildings, not merely in Russia, but in the world. It stands at one extremity of the "Red Square" in Moscow and close by one of the most celebrated entrances to the Kremlin, known as the Redeemer Gate. This church was erected by Ivan the Terrible about three hundred years ago over the grave of St. Basil, who was regarded as a popular prophet and miracle-worker at that time. The architecture of St. Basil's is amazing. From its roof rise eleven beautiful towers of different forms, crowned with cupolas resembling the turbans of oriental giants. The effect of its colouring can hardly be exaggerated. It is painted in all the colours of the rainbow, and its cupolas either sparkle with gold, or shine with brightly tinted tiles. Thus red, orange, purple, green, blue, violet, gold and silver are strangely blended here in one picturesque mass, like a fantastic castle made of prisms. When it was finished, Ivan the Terrible found it so remarkable, that he sent for the architect and asked him if he could ever build another such temple. The architect said "Yes." "That, by Heaven, you shall never do," cried Ivan, and caused his head to be immediately cut off. A cruel jealousy this, but exceedingly flattering to the architect.

INTERIOR OF GRAND OPERA HOUSE, PARIS.—If the exterior of this Temple of Music be imposing, the interior is dazzling. On a gala night the sight of its grand staircase, its balconies, corridors and magnificent foyer can never be forgotten. One pauses in bewilderment at the foot of this "Stairway of Honour." The steps are of white marble, the balustrades of alabaster, the hand-rail of African onyx. Twenty-four coloured marble columns rise to the height of the third floor. The ceiling glows with brilliant frescoes. Superb bronze groups surround us, bearing globes of light. At the head of the first landing, a doorway, flanked by enormous figures of Tragedy and Comedy, leads inward to the amphitheatre and orchestra. The pavements are of exquisite mosaic. The auditorium is open to the criticism of an excessive amount of gilded ornamentation, but the foyer, or promenading hall, is of extraordinary splendour. It is 177 feet long and 60 feet in height, and with its gilded columns, statues, paintings, marble chimney pieces and colossal mirrors, presents an appearance unsurpassed in any theatre in the world. The cost of this building, apart from that of its site, was about £1,400,000. It was begun in 1861 and opened in 1875, from the designs and under the directions of Garnier, whose name will thus be forever associated with the most gorgeous opera house that the world has yet produced.

THE TRANSFIGURATION (By RAPHAEL), ROME.—This wonderful picture represents two separate incidents. Below we see the crowd of people who have brought to nine of Christ's disciples the boy possessed of an evil spirit. The sight of this demoniac is painful. He is writhing in agony, supported by his anxious father who implores their aid. Two kneeling women also join their entreaties that the sufferer may be cured. The inability of the disciples to restore him is shown in their looks and gestures. Two of them point upward as if indicating the only source of help. Meanwhile the upper part of the picture represents Mt. Tabor. The three disciples who have accompanied their Master thither are lying prostrate, dazzled by the celestial radiance and shading their eyes from the miraculous brilliancy which confronts them. Above them in mid-air is the figure of Jesus, accompanied by Moses and Elias. The wonderfully serene and majestic expression on the face of Christ is perhaps the greatest charm of the entire painting. It is justly supposed that this picture was designed by Raphael not merely to portray the historical occurrence mentioned in the Gospels, but to symbolize the contrast between the joy and glory of Heaven and the sorrow and sufferings of earth. The great painter, who died at the youthful age of thirty-seven, was at work on this only a few days before his death, but had not quite completed it. It was therefore hung above the bed on which his body lay in state, and was borne through the streets of Rome in his funeral procession attended by an immense throng of weeping admirers and friends.

STATUE OF DAVID (BY MICHAEL ANGELO), FLORENCE.—This noble work by Italy's greatest sculptor stood formerly outside of the Palazzo Vecchio in the open Square of the Senate, where it had remained for centuries; but now it has been removed to a place of shelter for greater security. It is a figure of heroic size, like most of Michael Angelo's productions, and should be looked on from a little distance to be appreciated. As we observe its superb proportions and the stern and scrutinizing expression of the youthful David as he goes forth to battle with the Giant Goliath, whom he is evidently watching intently, we can not wonder that the advent of this statue was such an event in Florence, that for many years the Florentines would reckon special occurrences as happening "so long after the completion of the David!" It was the more remarkable since Michael Angelo had cut it from a block of marble eighteen feet in length, which had lain useless more than fifty years, no sculptor having dared to attack it. But Michael Angelo, struck with its beauty, and longing to achieve what others deemed impossible, resolved to carve from it a colossal statue representing the future King and Psalmist in the first great crisis of his life. People had up to that time been sceptical of Michael Angelo's genius; but when this figure was completed, there was no longer any doubt. He was the first living sculptor of the world!

THE IMMACULATE CONCEPTION (By Murillo), PARIS.—In the salon Carre of the Louvre, in Paris, hangs the masterpiece of the Spanish painter, Murillo. It represents the Virgin Mary as the very embodiment of youthful purity, innocence and beauty standing in the clouds and supported apparently by an immense throng of cherubs, who form below her and around her a perfect garland of childlike loveliness. Her upturned face, her rapturous expression, her folded hands, her robe of snowy whiteness, her exquisite blue mantle and her angelic retinue, all these form a wonderfully beautiful combination which has endeared this work of art to millions and will continue to do so while it still endures. Murillo has been called the "Painter of the Conception," for he is said to have portrayed this subject twenty-five times. His daughter, Francesca, often served him for a model. Other artists have usually represented the Virgin as a blonde. Murillo, on the contrary, portrayed her with dark hair and eyes, as is certainly more natural in an Oriental woman. A critic once said of this painting that those who did not know that Murillo had produced it would think it had had its origin in heaven. One must go to Spain, and above all to his native city, Seville, to fully appreciate Murillo's genius; for there are most of his wonderful paintings, which of themselves will well repay a trip to Spain. There he was beloved and admired during his life, and there he died on the 3d of April, 1682, from having fallen from a scaffolding while painting the "Marriage of St. Catherine."

THE CHURCH OF THE HOLY SEPULCHRE, JERUSALEM.—If the building in Jerusalem most revered by Moslems be the Mosque of Omar, the one most reverenced by Christians is the Church of the Holy Sepulchre. It is an enormous edifice, with no claims to architectural beauty, founded about 300 years after Christ by the Empress Helena, mother of Constantine, first of the Christian Emperors. In one sense it can hardly be called a *Church* at all. It is rather a sacred Exposition Building. Beneath its enormous roof are many chapels, altars, shrines, hills, caves, valleys and monuments, commemorating all the localities mentioned in the Bible which can by any possibility be situated in Jerusalem. Among the places supposed to be identified within the limits of this church, are the Sepulchre of Christ; the summit of Mt. Calvary; the places where Christ was scourged, crowned with thorns and anointed for burial; the spot where the true cross was found; the point where Jesus appeared to Mary Magdalene; the place where the Centurion stood during the crucifixion, and the grave of Adam! All these are the property of various Christian sects—Greeks, Latins, Armenians, Copts, Syrians and Abyssinians—all more or less jealous of each other and distrustful of each others' relics. Opinions of course differ as to the authenticity of these localities. But genuine or not, there is no doubt that the site of the Sepulchre itself has influenced the fate of Nations more than any other spot on earth. It caused the greatest event of the Middle Ages (the Crusades), and for its possession and defence the best and bravest blood in Christendom has been freely shed.

THE MOUNTAIN OF THE HOLY CROSS, COLORADO.—Solemn and awful in its isolation from the lower world there rises in the heart of the Rocky Mountains a weird and most impressive peak upon which many an eye has looked with superstitious reverence. For there in lines of crystal clearness, and visible for many miles away, Nature has traced the form of a gigantic cross. Two monstrous fissures in the mountain's side so intersect each other at right angles as to produce this beautiful phenomenon. It is invariably radiant with the dawn hours before the morning mists have left the valleys, and long after the shades of evening have fallen on the lower hills, with outstretched arms that mighty cross seems giving to the sleepy world its benediction. The Mountain of the Holy Cross is not so high as some of its companions, yet it has an altitude of 14,000 feet, and its extraordinary appearance makes it unique among the mountains of the world. Moreover, its ascent is exceedingly difficult and dangerous. But how sublime the prospect when the ascent is made! How few Americans as yet realize what scenery is here outspread for their enjoyment! In Colorado alone there is a magnificent mountain chain embracing an area of *hundreds of square miles*, and abounding in wonderful cañons, valleys, lakes and rivers, above which tower snow-clad summits rivalling and even surpassing the most famous monarchs of the Alps.

VENDOME COLUMN, PARIS.—Rising from the very heart of Paris stands this sombre shaft of bronze, recalling the career of the great Napoleon. The Emperor was fond of rearing monuments in the style of the old Romans. This is in imitation of the Column of Trajan at Rome. On both those shafts, the Roman and the French, are plates of bronze adorned with figures in relief ascending toward the summit in a spiral path. In this Vendome Column not only do these figures represent events in Bonaparte's campaign of Austerlitz, but the bronze for the plates themselves was made by melting down 1,200 Austrian and Russian cannon. Upon the summit, 142 feet high, stands the statue of Napoleon I. This is not, however, the figure originally placed there. When the Emperor had been banished to St. Helena, the Royalists took down his statue and crowned the shaft with a gigantic fleur-de-lis. But this decoration was, under the circumstances, so senseless that the Napoleonic figure was restored. The Communists in their endeavour to ruin Paris actually pulled down this column in 1871, but happily the fragments were preserved and it was re-erected in 1875. The name "Vendome" was given to this shaft because the square in which it stands was called the Place Vendome, from a palace which once stood here, owned by the Duke of Vendome, a son of Henry IV.

NIAGARA FALLS.—Niagara is too sublime a subject for minute description. The mighty overflow of Lakes Superior, Huron, Michigan and Erie, here makes a leap of 167 feet—magnificent in volume, dazzling in radiance, stupendous in its breadth and awe-inspiring in its ceaseless roar. Of all word-painting of this scene which man has ever tried, nothing surpasses these appropriate phrases of Charles Dickens: "It was not till I came to *Table Rock* and looked—Great Heavens!—on *what* a fall of bright green water, that it all flashed upon me in its might and majesty. Then when I felt how near to my Creator I was standing, the first impression and the lasting one of this tremendous spectacle was—*Peace*; calm recollections of the Dead; great thoughts of an eternal rest and happiness! E'en now in many a quiet hour I think, Still do those waters roar and rush, and leap and tumble all day long! Still are the rainbows spanning them one hundred feet below! Still, when the sun is on them, do they shine like molten gold; still, when the day is gloomy, do they seem to crumble like a great chalk cliff, or like a mass of dense, white smoke. But ever does the mighty stream appear to *die*, as it descends, and from its grave rises that ghost of mist and spray, which never has been laid, but which still haunts the place with the same dread solemnity as when the First Flood, *Light*, came rushing on Creation at the word of God!"

HOUSES OF PARLIAMENT, LONDON.—These noble buildings are worthy of their fame. The finest view of them is obtained thus from the river, along the embankment of which they extend for 940 feet. Built in elaborate Gothic style, their ornamentations including graceful towers, pinnacles, fluted columns, interesting statues, and a bewildering amount of fine stone carving relieve the enormous structure of monotony. This edifice covers an area of eight acres. The rooms which it contains are numbered by hundreds, and its corridors can be reckoned by miles. The grand "Victoria Tower" at the southern end of the building reaches the imposing height of 340 feet, and is more than seventy feet square. Through this the Queen enters when she opens Parliament, on which occasion the flag of England is always displayed above the tower. The clock tower at the northern end of these Imperial legislative halls is only twenty feet lower than its rival. Each of its four great dials measures ninety-two feet in circumference. The minute hand is a bar of steel more than twelve feet in length! It is said that five hours are required to wind it up. Every one who has spent a night in London must have heard the great bell of this tower proclaim the flight of time in deep and solemn tones, which are to those of other bells like the voice of an organ to the sound of a piano. This bell, which weighs no less than thirteen tons, is known as "Big Ben," and for years had no rival. But now it is surpassed by the new monster recently placed in St. Paul's Cathedral. Still they are far enough apart to make no interference with each other. The kingdom of "Big Ben" has simply been curtailed. Over this part of gigantic London he still reigns supreme.

PALACE OF FONTAINEBLEAU, FRANCE.—This is one of the most interesting as well as the most elegantly decorated of all the Chateaux of France. Situated about forty miles from Paris, it was the favourite residence of Francis I. (died 1547), of Henry IV. (died 1610), and particularly of the first Napoleon. Here for some months he kept Pope Pius VII. his prisoner. Here, after the long and deadly duel between France and Europe, he signed his abdication in 1814; and one may see the room in which in his despair he attempted then to commit suicide by taking poison prepared for him during the Russian campaign. The palace courtyard has associated with itself some most pathetic souvenirs. It is called the "Court of the Adieux," because it was here that Napoleon, on the 20th of April, 1814, after his abdication, said farewell to his Old Guard. It was at the hour of noon that a solitary figure appeared at the head of the main staircase and descended its steps to meet his faithful grenadiers. It was the figure of Napoleon about to depart into exile. Embracing one or two of the officers, and pressing the "Eagle" of France repeatedly to his lips, he uttered to his Old Guard those impressive words of farewell with which every reader of French history is familiar. Then amid the sobs of his old soldiers, who were faithful to him in adversity as in prosperity, unlike so many whom the Emperor had enriched with honours, titles and estates, Napoleon (once more apparently their "Little Corporal") entered a carriage and was driven away from this palace where he had been so recently the most powerful sovereign in the world.

GALLERY OF HENRY II., PALACE OF FONTAINEBLEAU, FRANCE.—The interior of the palace of Fontainebleau is of great magnificence, and the gallery of Henry Second, outlined in this illustration, is one of the richest of all its historic halls. It was begun by Francis I., embellished by Henry II., and restored by Louis Philippe. This was the great reception
room of Fontainebleau, and at intervals in the decorations of the walls and ceilings we see the letters H. and D., the initials of Henry II. and the beautiful Diana of Poitiers. The chimney-
piece in this apartment is one of the most elegant in Europe. In connection with the exterior of this palace, allusion has been made to some of its Napoleonic souvenirs, but many other
associations give to it historical importance. Here in 1685 Louis XIV. signed the Revocation of the Edict of Nantes, by which nearly a century before Henry IV. had granted toleration to
the Protestants. Here the beautiful and ill-fated Marie Antoinette at times resided. Here, while a guest at the French Court in 1657, Queen Christiana of Sweden caused her former
favourite, Count Monaldeschi, to be put to death. Here also Louis XV. was married, and the subsequent Napoleon III. was baptized; and one may see the room within this palace where the
sentence of divorce was pronounced against the Empress Josephine in 1809. From the windows of this splendid apartment one looks out over a pretty park towards the famous Forest of
Fontainebleau, threaded with charming walks and drives, and covering an area about fifty miles in circumference.

THE ALBERT MEMORIAL, LONDON.—One of the most magnificent monuments in the world is the structure outlined in this illustration. It is the "Albert Memorial," erected to the memory of the Prince Consort (husband of Queen Victoria), partly by the Government and partly by voluntary contributions at a cost of £120,000. The very foundation of this monument alone repays an hour's close examination. Broad granite steps lead up on every side to a spacious platform, at the four corners of which are fine colossal groups of statuary, representing the four great divisions of our globe, Europe, Asia, Africa and America. The pedestal itself is nothing less than wonderful in its elaborate display of marble statues in relief encircling the entire monument. There are 169 of these figures, representing the world's greatest artists since the dawn of history, including Painters, Musicians, Poets, Architects, Sculptors, Heroes and Reformers. In one place, for example, Homer, the Father of Poetry, is portrayed, holding the lyre, while near to him in attitudes of reverent attention are Virgil, Dante, Shakespeare, Cervantes, Milton and Boccaccio. In another section are grouped Michael Angelo, Donatello, John of Bologna, Benvenuto Cellini, and other sculptors of the Renaissance. At last above all this rises to the height of 175 feet a gorgeously decorated Gothic canopy, beneath which is seated a colossal statue of the Prince Consort, fifteen feet in height and made of gilded bronze. The excessive amount of ornamentation in mosaic and gilding on this canopy may be criticized, but there is no doubt of the grand and imposing effect produced by the lower portion of this superb memorial.

BRANDENBURG GATE, BERLIN.—This fine historic portal of Berlin forms the commencement of its most famous street, the "Unter den Linden," or "Under the Lime Trees." Its situation thus is admirable, for the avenue which it adorns is straight as an arrow and a mile in length. Accordingly, this Gate is visible at a great distance. It is decidedly imposing, being about 70 feet in height and 200 in breadth. It is perforated by five different passageways, the central one being reserved for carriages of royalty. Upon the summit is a bronze car of Victory drawn by four horses. It has had a remarkable history. In 1806 when Napoleon passed beneath this gate as conqueror of Prussia, he ordered that this triumphal chariot should be sent to Paris to adorn one of his own arches of triumph there. But after Napoleon's downfall the Prussians brought it back with shouts of rejoicing, restored the Goddess of Victory to her throne on the Brandenburg Gate, and named the square on which she looks exultingly "The Place of Paris." In 1871 beneath this arch a large portion of the German army, together with the Emperor, Crown Prince and Bismarck, re-entered Berlin amid the wildest enthusiasm after the war with France. Beyond this gateway is the famous park of Berlin, the Thiergarten, and every afternoon this portal is the nucleus of much of the display of Berlin's gay and fashionable life, as handsome carriages roll outward to the pleasure-grounds or inward toward the city.

BEACH OF SCHEVENINGEN, HOLLAND.—Only a few miles distant from the Hague is this most fashionable of Holland watering-places. Between the city and this beach horse-cars and omnibuses are in constant motion. On warm summer days the entire population of the capital seems to have assembled on these sands. There is, however, a very different kind of life led on this beach during the greater part of the year. The pleasure-seekers depart with the first cold autumnal storm, but the quaint fishing people of Scheveningen remain, permanent features of the landscape. Living within three miles of the capital, and every summer invaded by the crowds of fashion, they nevertheless preserve unchanged the primitive habits and dress of their forefathers. Their costumes are exceedingly odd and amusing. Their faces appear old and anxious. Nor is this strange. For what a toilsome, cheerless life they lead during a greater part of the year, when only the old men, women and children are left to watch and wait, and keep the hearth-stone bright, while all the stalwart men of the village are at sea! But when the fleet comes back, then is there joy indeed, and great excitement attends the landing and public sale of fish upon the shore. As one walks upon this beach, watching its angry waves, and realizing that large portions of Holland are below the ocean level, he thinks with admiration of the courage and eternal vigilance of this sturdy nation, which holds the sea at bay, and whose very existence is a splendid proof of man's superiority over Nature.

BOULEVARD ANSPACH, BRUSSELS, BELGIUM.—Brussels is a bright, cheerful city, as Belgium, of which it is the capital, is a pretty, richly cultivated and interesting land. Of all the countries of Europe, none equal Belgium in the average of population to the area, there being about four hundred here to the square mile. So thickly covered is it with cities and villages that Philip II. said of it that it was only one large town. Each of its cities has some interesting features, historic souvenirs or works of art; but Brussels naturally surpasses them all. Some of its streets, like this displayed in the illustration, are thoroughly modern and Parisian in their appearance; but there are others lined with quaint and picturesque mediæval buildings, reminding us of former scenes of gaiety and splendour, tragedy and woe. At one turn we may see some stately structure of the present, like the Bourse or Palace of Justice, and at the next behold the Hotel de Ville, within which was being celebrated the ball on the eve of the battle of Waterloo, immortalized by Byron in Childe Harold. Waterloo is in fact only ten miles from Brussels, and the tourist who strolls idly along this handsome boulevard can, if he will, go thence in an hour to that fatal field where the Man of Destiny received his death-blow, and from which he began the mournful path to St. Helena. As an illustration of the way in which the modern and the ancient mingle here in Brussels, it may be remembered that now in its most fashionable square rises the statue of the old hero, Godfrey de Bouillon, to commemorate the place where he summoned the populace to join him in the grand Crusade to recover the Holy Sepulchre.

HOF-BURG THEATRE, VIENNA.—Everyone has heard of the magnificent Opera House of Vienna, which for years has had the reputation of being, all things considered, the World's best Temple of Music. But that edifice has now a dangerous rival in the new Imperial Theatre, represented in this illustration. It is another of those architectural jewels which sparkle in the glittering girdle that now divides in two concentric parts the Austrian capital, and which in another illustration has been described as the "Ring Strassen," or Circular Boulevards. This beautiful structure is the favoured home of the Drama, as the Opera House is the abode of Music in Vienna, and no city in the world can boast of two such structures devoted to this purpose. Paris alone can claim a richer Opera House, but even Paris has no theatre comparable to this which rises thus in stately grandeur on the Ring Strassen. Everything here is managed with perfect order and good taste. Before and after the performance polite uniformed officials stand on the steps to assist the visitors to alight. Once past the marble corridor, one finds a number of ticket offices to obviate all crowding. The cloak rooms, too, are large, with numerous attendants to prevent delay; while courteous ushers lead the way into a most richly decorated auditorium. This theatre is of course subsidized by the Government, and only dramas of the highest order are here given, while the style in which they are produced is well worthy of the magnificent structure itself.

CASTLE OF SAN ANGELO AND TIBER, ROME.—One of the most beautiful and impressive views of Rome is that represented in this illustration, embracing the Tiber, the Castle of San Angelo, and in the distance the majestic dome of St. Peter's. For amid all the changes that have swept over Rome, one thing at least remains comparatively unchanged. It is this yellow, legend-laden Tiber, still rolling on with tawny waves beneath its arches toward the setting sun, and guarding deeply in its breast some of the mightiest memories of the world. How many lives, for example, it has remorselessly engulfed—from those of brave defenders of the city to countless victims of Imperial or Papal tyranny! And, oh! what treasures no doubt lurk within its sands! The Castle of San Angelo is not the name which seems appropriate to this huge circular structure which casts its sombre shadow in the stream beneath. That is a title bestowed upon it by Pope Gregory the Great; but, in reality, that building is the grand Mausoleum of Hadrian, erected by that monarch as his place of sepulture 1,700 years ago. Now it is bare and desolate, but once its curving wall was covered with pure Parian marble and decorated with the finest Grecian statues and Corinthian columns, destined, alas! to be hurled down upon the heads of an invading army of Barbarians, who nevertheless were ultimately successful and threw with brutal laughter to the Tiber's waves the ashes of Marcus Aurelius Antoninus and Hadrian himself.

THE RIALTO, VENICE.—That which stirs the pulse more than all else upon this Grand Canal is the famous bridge of the Rialto ; built entirely of white marble and consisting of a single arch one hundred and fifty-eight feet in length.   It is worth a month of ordinary life to have the privilege of bidding our gondolier halt beneath this bridge, thronged with the memories of three hundred years, and floating there to let the tide of historic associations sweep over us.   For environed as we are by all that make these memories real, we think of Shylock and Othello and of the old Doges who ruled here in magnificence for one thousand years !   We think of the time when, just as this bridge unites the eastern and the western banks of this canal, so Venice itself was the connecting link between Europe and Asia, and held for years in her controlling hands the commerce of the civilized world.   Moreover, almost in the shadow of this marble arch appeared the first bank of deposit which the world had known ; in Venice also was published the first book ever printed in Italy ; while on this very bridge was sold the first newspaper ever published in the world, which (bartered for a coin called Gazetta) has given a name to many of our modern journals.   Nor can we here forget how Venice, in her glorious career of conquest, once caused her standard to roll out its purple folds over some of the richest islands in the Mediterranean and Adriatic.

SORRENTO, ITALY.—On the southern shore of the enchanting and incomparable Bay of Naples lies the village of Sorrento. To reach it from Naples one rides along a winding road cut in the brow of cliffs two hundred or three hundred feet in height, which constitute a glorious frame for that lovely mirror which holds reflected in itself visions of surpassing beauty! These wave-washed bluffs are covered with villas, convents, groves and gardens which become especially numerous and attractive on and about the wooded point projecting from the shore and called Sorrento. It is no exaggeration to say that in the spring and autumn this is a perfect paradise of beauty; for it is surrounded with orange and lemon groves gleaming with shining leaves and fruit of gold. As one inhales here the soft air laden with the breath of blossoms and hears the choirs of nightingales which chant here through the spring, he realizes that his youthful dreams have been fulfilled, and that at last ITALY seems all that he fondly fancied it in childhood! The hotels of Sorrento line the cliff which overhangs the sea, and behind them are luxuriant gardens and orange groves. The population of the place is quite prosperous, being chiefly engaged in straw-plaiting, lace-making or olive wood carving, in which they are proficient. It was in Sorrento that the poet Tasso was born, in a house now used as a hotel, from which the view over the Bay towards Naples and the islands of Capri and Ischia is indescribably beautiful.

PIAZZA CARLO ALBERTO, TURIN, ITALY.—One of the brightest and most cheerful of Italian cities is Turin, which from 1859 to 1865 was the capital of Italy and the residence of the King. Its spacious squares, broad streets, numerous gardens and fine public buildings make it a very agreeable town to visit, although it can not boast of so many priceless souvenirs of art and history as its sister cities of Italy possess. Nevertheless, Turin is ancient, for it was founded by the Emperor Augustus 1900 years ago; and it was in recent times the principal centre of those national struggles which resulted in the unification of Italy. It is the birth-place of the illustrious statesman, Cavour, and a magnificent monument has been erected here in his honour. Here also was born King Victor Emanuel, whose statues and monuments also decorate the city. The building seen in the illustration is the Palazzo Carignano, which was the Sardinian Chamber of Deputies till 1860, and after that for five years was the Hall of the Italian Parliament. The bronze equestrian statue in front of it is that of King Carlo Alberto, for whom the square is named. The pedestal is approached by four steps of Scottish granite; at the corners stand as a faithful body-guard four colossal statues of Sardinian soldiers; and above are four female figures representing Freedom, Justice, Independence and Patriotism. Among the objects of interest which Turin offers to the traveller are the *Royal Armoury*, containing many valuable relics of various celebrated soldiers from Charles V. down to Napoleon I., an admirable *Picture Gallery*, and the *National Museum*, which is the loftiest structure in Europe with the exception of the Eiffel Tower in Paris, its height being 538 feet.

THE PIRAEUS, ATHENS, GREECE.—No traveller who has the least admiration for classical associations can gaze upon this port of Athens without profound emotion. It still retains its ancient name of the Piraeus, and on these waves, which are as blue to-day as when they charmed the eyes of Socrates or Xenophon, Athenian ships once rode at anchor, and many a fleet has swept hence into the Ægean for some glorious victory. How strange it seems, on landing here, to read upon the shops and corners of the streets words in those old Greek characters which we learned in boyhood! It all sweeps back upon us. The modern city fades from view, and in its place the traveller sees the school-room with its rows of well-worn desks. He feels again upon his cheek the summer breeze, as it came in temptingly through the open window, and lured him from his Greek lexicon to the fair fields. At last Xenophon's graphic style and Homer's matchless verse seem based upon reality. Six miles from the Piraeus is Athens itself, and in the clear atmosphere of Attica its famous hill, the temple-crowned Acropolis, is plainly visible, as are its adjoining mountains, Pentelicus, Hymettus and Lycabettus. Interesting, therefore, as this Athenian harbour is in some respects, it is only a doorway to glories beyond, and after leaving his steamer here the tourist is eager to hasten on to the capital itself, thronged with inspiring memories and still retaining traces of those works of art which have made Athens immortal. At the Piraeus, therefore, one justly feels that he is standing on the threshold of one of the most interesting countries in the world, and that it is all before him to enjoy, first in its glorious historical associations, second in the excitement of actual sight-seeing, and lastly in the calmer but perpetual pleasure of its retrospection.

CAIRO, LOOKING TOWARDS THE CITADEL.—Measured by the vast antiquity possessed by many Egyptian monuments and cities, Cairo is comparatively modern, although it has been the capital of Egypt more than one thousand years. When the foundations of its walls were being laid, the planet Mars, which the Arabs call Kahir, or "the Victorious," crossed the meridian of the new city. Accordingly the Caliph called it "Kahira," from which the word *Cairo* is derived. In 1166 the Citadel (visible in this illustration and elsewhere described) was built by the famous warrior Saladin. During the reigns of this Caliph and many of his successors, Cairo was beautifully adorned with mosques, palaces and tombs, which even in their partial ruin at the present time are striking proofs of the delicacy and grace of Saracenic architecture. Napoleon I. left here some traces of his path of conquest, for in 1798, after the Battle of the Pyramids, the future Emperor of the French established his headquarters at Cairo. Cairo is the largest city in Africa, and the second city in the whole Turkish empire. Its population is about 400,000. No other Oriental city offers so much to entertain and instruct the traveller. Not only do its street scenes afford an endless fund of amusement by interpreting in actual life the stories of the "Arabian Nights," but close beside this charming capital are the oldest relics of human workmanship upon the surface of our globe. Thus within a few miles of Cairo are the Pyramids, the Sphinx, and the sites of some of the oldest cities in the world, Memphis and Heliopolis. Beyond the Nile, and in full view from the platform of the Citadel, is the vast Desert of Sahara, extending for hundreds of miles to the westward; and in the city itself is a marvellous collection of souvenirs of the days of the Pharaohs. Cairo is also, of course, the starting point of the delightful journey up the Nile in steamers or in private boats.

SCENE OF THE CRUCIFIXION, PASSION PLAY, OBERAMMERGAU.—The village of Oberammergau, hidden away in the Tyrolese Alps of Bavaria, lies for nine years lifeless and forgotten. Then every tenth year it suddenly emerges from its obscurity, and, like a comet at its periodic visitation, comes once more into the vision of mankind. The cause of this celebrity at the recurrence of each decade is the performance there of its wonderful Passion Play. Two hundred and fifty years ago a plague was raging in Bavaria. In Oberammergau alone one hundred persons had thus perished. The terrified survivors made a vow to God that if He would thereafter spare their lives they would henceforth perform every ten years a drama of Christ's life and sufferings. The plague abated, and ever since those villagers have deemed themselves compelled to carry out the vow of their forefathers, bequeathing it from generation to generation as a sacred and important legacy. Elsewhere the Passion Play would seem offensive. Like a wild mountain-flower, it would not bear transplanting to another soil. In Oberammergau, however, it is appropriate and natural. The piety, sincerity and intelligence of these villagers, who profit by centuries of stage-tradition and are filled with enthusiasm and religious fervour, reconcile even the most sensitive to this remarkable production. The play is performed every Sunday (and sometimes oftener) through the months of June, July, August and September. It lasts from eight in the morning till six in the evening, with the intermission of an hour and a half at noon. It has eighteen acts and twenty-five tableaux. Sometimes five hundred people are on the stage at once. Joseph Maier, who for three decades has enacted the part of Christ, is a man of noble character, majestic figure and positive genius in his refined conception of his role. The scene of the Crucifixion is the most thrilling in the drama. Maier hangs upon the cross for twenty-two minutes, and all the details narrated in the Gospels are faithfully carried out. To see these various incidents thus solemnly and beautifully represented under the open sky, as if in actual life, is a unique experience, repaying almost any sacrifice. Forever after it lingers in the memory like a benediction.

NEW MORMON TEMPLE, UTAH.—Salt Lake City is in some respects the most extraordinary settlement that men have ever founded. It has a population of about 35,000 people. Its streets are lined with many handsome buildings. Business is active there. It is in many ways a city of the world, like any other great metropolis. Yet no one enters it without perceiving traces of that Mormon religion, which founded here in 1847 this "City of Saints," and still exerts upon its life so powerful an influence. Over most of the shops is the motto, "Holiness to the Lord," and we learn that the church regulates those merchants' prices and receives from them a percentage on all sales. Almost every house has its little garden of fruit and shade trees. On each side of the principal streets runs a crystalline stream of water coming from the mountains. Two famous buildings stand near the centre of the city. One is the Tabernacle, of whose huge dome, vast auditorium and wonderful acoustic properties all the world has heard. But even the Tabernacle is destined to be surpassed by the *Temple* represented in this illustration. It is a structure which at once commands our admiration by its immense dimensions and massive grandeur. Its walls of sparkling polished granite are one hundred feet in height, and its towers are to rise one hundred feet higher still. It is emphatically "fire-proof," for its walls of solid granite are eight feet thick, and the partition walls, floors and ceilings are also of solid stone. Its foundations are sixteen feet thick. The corner-stone of this imposing structure was laid in 1853, but the Temple is not yet completed. It has already cost £500,000.

ROTTERDAM, HOLLAND.—This famous centre of Dutch commerce lies fourteen miles from the North Sea, at the union of two rivers, one of which gives to the town its name. For this stream is called the Rotter, and a great dyke or dam erected here bestows upon the place the title of Rotter-dam! This is indeed a clue by which to comprehend all similar Dutch names. Thus Amsterdam signifies the dam upon the Amstel; and so it is with Schiedam, Zaandam, Edam, Durgerdam, Volendam and all the other *dams*. But since every public square in Holland is also called a Dam; and since the tram-car signs are always telling us of this Dam or that Dam; and since in the construction of their dykes the Dutch have constantly to use the coffer-dam; if any country in the world may be said without profanity to be effectually "dammed," Holland is the one. In Rotterdam one always sees a multitude of bridges. From almost any point you can count eight or ten; and since most of them are draw-bridges, they keep rising and falling like parts of an immense machine. Some of the boats which we see on the canals of Rotterdam are actually employed in bringing *water* to the city! This seems like taking coals to Newcastle, but, notwithstanding its aqueous surroundings, Rotterdam, like most of Holland cities, has no abundance of good *drinking* water. Perhaps it is not strange therefore that not far away is a thriving town whose 300 distilleries produce the world-renowned Holland gin, which is familiarly known as "Hollands."

MUSEUMS AND STATUE OF MARIA THERESA, VIENNA.—Just off the handsome curving boulevards of Vienna called the "Ring Strassen," are two imposing structures almost the exact counterparts of each other in form, decorations and dimensions. They are the new Imperial Museums just completed at a cost of over a million pounds. One is to contain the famous Belvedere picture gallery and other great collections scattered through the city; while its companion edifice will be devoted to ARCHAEOLOGY and NATURAL HISTORY—forming together thus one of the finest collections of Art and Science in the world. Within the centre of this square, between these New Museums, is an elaborate monument in bronze erected recently to the memory of the Empress Maria Theresa. It is designed to commemorate her entire reign. Below the statue of the Empress are reliefs portraying prominent events connected with her history; beneath these are fine statues of her ablest statesmen; while on the corners are equestrian figures of her leading generals. Well may Austria honour thus the most illustrious sovereign that ever occupied her throne. It would be hard to find in history a woman who had more imperial qualities and sterling character than Maria Theresa. For she was brave as well as beautiful, and dauntless as she was devout. It was for her that her chivalric Hungarian nobles with drawn swords exclaimed as with one voice, "Let us die for our KING, Maria Theresa."

NAPOLEON'S CARRIAGE, VERSAILLES.—Among the relics of royalty and of the empire displayed at Versailles is this magnificent vehicle, the woodwork of which is one mass of gilding, while the interior decorations are of the most elegant description. This is said to be the carriage in which the Emperor Napoleon I. went with the Empress Marie Louise to solemnize their marriage in the Cathedral of Notre Dame. All Paris was in the greatest excitement, and Napoleon's future seemed then brilliant beyond all precedent in modern history. Yet in reality these gilded wheels were swiftly bearing him to what Napoleon himself subsequently called "an abyss covered with flowers." And such indeed proved to be this fatal marriage following his divorce from Josephine. No doubt Napoleon's pride was gratified, as in this gorgeous vehicle he sat beside his Austrian bride, but it was certainly impossible for him to ever love her as he had once loved Josephine. The latter, slightly older than himself, had been his life-long confidant and friend. She had at first contributed much to his success. Her intuitions made her a most useful counsellor. But what was Marie Louise? A simple, inexperienced girl, with whom the Emperor always wore a mask, lest his designs should through her reach the court of Austria! The one possessed a character as weak and vacillating as her face would indicate. The other proved herself a heroine by sacrificing to the interests of France not only the most enviable throne in Europe, but also the most famous of earth's sovereigns, and the man she loved. "It will not bring him fortune," said the common people when the divorce had been proclaimed; and they were right.

THE CHURCH OF ST. MARK, VENICE.—The Church of St. Mark has stood here for nearly eight hundred years as a splendid proof of the ancient magnificence of Venice. Its architecture is most extraordinary. With its bulbous domes and minaret-like belfries, its glittering mosaics, and cupolas sparkling with gold, it seems more like a Mohammedan than a Christian shrine. One might also call it a Christian mosque! The Venetians brought back with them from their Eastern wars ideas of Oriental architecture which pleased them, but in attempting to repeat them they made a singular medley of the whole. Yet no expense was spared to make it magnificent. For, to say nothing of its splendid columns and rich carving, the mosaics on its *exterior* alone cover an area of 45,790 square feet, and are still gorgeous in their golden and purple colours. And when we think that this is nothing to the vast expanse of mosaic *within*, we are no longer surprised that this sanctuary has been proudly called "La Chiesa Aurea," or the Church of Gold, and compared to a cavern hung with stalactites of precious stones! During more than five centuries, the first question addressed to generals and captains returning from the Eastern wars was this: "What new and splendid offering bring you for San Marco?" Above the doorway of this famous church are four enormous horses made of gilded bronze. They were originally in Rome, and adorned Nero's golden chariot of the Sun. From Rome they were taken by Constantine to Constantinople. Thence they were brought by the conquering Doges to Venice. Napoleon I. also took them to Paris; but after Waterloo they were restored by the allies to the Queen of the Adriatic.

HARBOUR OF ALEXANDRIA, EGYPT.—The coast of Egypt is not particularly striking as one approaches it. No hills or mountains rise above its sandy shore. The light-house at Alexandria seems in consequence unusually lofty, and recalls to us the ancient Pharos of this port, which was reckoned as one of the seven wonders of the world, and from the top of which the fire kept burning constantly at night could be seen miles away at sea. This harbour is usually filled with a multitude of ships and steamers, since this is not merely the great seaport of Egypt, but an important city in itself, through which Egyptian exports find their principal outlet. Of these the most important are cotton and cotton-seed, wheat, coffee, elephants' tusks, ostrich feathers and mother-of-pearl. Regular steamboat services and two telegraphic cables connect Alexandria with Europe, while railroads and the telegraph place it in close communication with the whole of Egypt. Something of the maritime traffic of this city has declined since the opening of the Suez Canal and the prominence given to Port Said at its junction with the Mediterranean; but Alexandria even now contains a population of 200,000, and 50,000 European residents here prove the commercial value of this portal of the country of the Nile.

CAPE TOWN, SOUTH AFRICA.—This Capital of the British possessions in South Africa lies at the foot of Table Mountain on the shore of Table Bay. It was founded by the Dutch in 1650, but in 1795 was taken, together with the colony, by the English. At the peace of Amiens it was restored to the Dutch, but in 1806 it was once more taken by the English and has since remained in their possession. The town is quite regularly built; the houses are of good size and are mostly of brick or stone, generally having a veranda in front. The town is exposed to great heat, facing the noon-day sun and backed by naked mountains. The Castle is on the right side of the town and commands the anchorage of Table Bay. Many of the public offices of the Colony are within the fortress and its walls also contain barracks holding 1,000 men. Table Bay is capable of containing a great number of ships, but it is exposed to a very heavy swell during the prevalence of the westerly winds in June, July and August, though at other times it affords safe anchorage. An observatory has been built about two miles north of the town and large iron buildings have been erected as depots for coal to supply steamers touching at Cape Town en route to Australia. Table Mountain at the height of 900 feet is a solid mass of granite, but after ascending 900 feet more it changes to red sandstone. Its entire height is 3,567 feet above the sea.

IMPERIAL PALACE OF BEYLERBEY, ON THE BOSPHORUS, TURKEY.—It is difficult to imagine anything more charming than the scenery along the Bosphorus, where the opposite banks of Europe and Asia for fifteen miles coquettishly advance towards each other and then retreat, in a delightful series of undulating, wooded hills. These headlands of the two great continents are at times so near to each other that a person standing on one side of the Bosphorus can make himself heard by anyone on the opposite bank. Moreover these winding shores are lined with a constant succession of villages, pavilions, mosques and palaces, embosomed often in luxuriant foliage. From almost any of these places the views of the other shore and of the Bosphorus itself studded with snowy sails are of great loveliness. Here also are several charming pleasure-resorts for the people of Constantinople, among which are the "Sweet Waters" of Europe and Asia. On one prominent promontory is the admirable American school, Robert College, which gives a thorough education to more than 200 students. There are several palaces and villas of the Sultan along the Bosphorus, one of which is represented in this illustration. This palace of Beylerbey is used chiefly as a summer-residence, or as an elegantly furnished dwelling to be placed at the disposal of any royal guests of the Turkish Sovereign. The little town about it was under the Byzantine Emperors distinguished by the size and splendour of its edifices. For every portion of both sides of the Bosphorus is historic ground, and it is still emphatically true that "Earth hath no fairer sight to show, Than this blue strait, whose waters flow, Bordered with vineyards, summer bowers, White palaces and ivied towers."

STATION, RAMLEH, PALESTINE.—On the direct route from Jaffa to Jerusalem is the town of Ramleh, which is said to occupy the site of the ancient Arimathea. Under the Arabs in the ninth and tenth centuries it was a prosperous and important place, and was larger than Jerusalem itself. To-day it contains about 3,000 inhabitants, of whom 1,000 are Christians of the Greek Church. There is an old Latin monastery here where travellers are lodged and fed with comparative comfort. A lofty tower also rises above the town and once formed part of an enormous Mosque. The country around Ramleh is remarkably fertile. The vegetation is luxuriant. Olive trees abound, and with proper cultivation the fields in this part of Palestine could produce crops of which any country might be proud. The most astounding innovation here in recent times has been the *railroad*, which has already advanced beyond Ramleh and will eventually connect Jaffa with Jerusalem, thirty-three miles away! Within a short time, therefore, the old methods of horse-back riding and carriages over this part of the Holy Land will be discarded. A locomotive will transport tourists across the plains of Sharon; a railroad bridge will span the brook where David chose the smooth stones for his conflict with Goliath; and the porters may call out to passengers, "Ramleh, residence of Joseph of Arimathea. Five minutes for refreshments!" On the ground of sentiment, however, most people will regret to have a locomotive's whistle wake the echoes of Mount Zion. Here it is the old which interests us, not the new; and railways seem unsuited to the land of Abraham.

BRIDGE OF SHOPS, SRINAGAR, INDIA.—Srinagar is the capital of Cashmere, that valley in the Himalaya mountains so famous for its beauty, and which is represented in an adjoining illustration. It has a population of 135,000 people, and is built for four miles on both banks of the river Jhelum, which here is a placid stream with a breadth of about 300 feet. This river is crossed by many wooden bridges, lined with decayed and weather-beaten shops and houses, most of which are adorned with balconies and lattice windows. Some have their upper stories propped up by poles, and look decidedly insecure, as they overhang either the narrow streets or the river itself. The town is also intersected with innumerable canals, and from this fact and from its beautiful situation, Srinagar has been called the Venice of Asia. That is enough, however, to make the old Venetian Doges turn in their graves! For this Indian city is really too filthy and dilapidated to be seriously compared to the Queen of the Adriatic. Yet it possesses some Hindoo temples and an enormous mosque in which it is said that 60,000 people can worship at once. There was a time, however, when this capital of Cashmere was of great importance. It was a favourite resort of the old Mogul emperors, many of whose palaces are still standing in its vicinity. One of these Moore selected for his closing scene of Lalla Rookh. Even now Srinagar has some commercial prominence, for it is the centre of the shawl manufacture of Cashmere.

TEMPLE OF THE 500 GODS, CANTON, CHINA.—One of the most celebrated of all the hundreds of temples and pagodas in the city of Canton is that which contains 500 gilded statues of deified warriors, heroes, sages and apostles of the Buddhist faith. It looks more like a gallery of sculpture than a place of worship, with these long lines of solemn-looking figures staring each other out of countenance century after century! They certainly are not praiseworthy as works of art, yet incense is burnt constantly before some of them, and the air is heavy with that pungent perfume. China is a land of shrines and prayers. Even the shops of Canton have little altars at their doors dedicated to the God of Wealth, that deity who is in one way or another universally worshipped in all countries! In America it goes under the name of the Almighty Dollar. The Chinese deities, it would seem, are largely composed of departed and distinguished ancestors. Reverence for parents is one of the important precepts in China, and the result is that filial reverence and obedience are characteristic traits of the Chinese. These sentiments extend even beyond the grave, so that when parents die, prayers are addressed to them as to guardian spirits. Benevolent societies are therefore numerous in Chinese cities, so that poor or suffering relatives may be tenderly cared for. Thus orphan asylums, homes for the aged and infirm, and public hospitals exist here, not as copies of European institutions, but having been maintained in China for many centuries. Some good features can be found in almost every race and every religion, however widely they may differ from our own.

HEXAGONAL TEMPLE, KIOTO, JAPAN.—Kioto is called the City of Temples, and it well deserves the name. The traveller sees so many, that it is ever after difficult for him to recall them separately. They are of various shapes and sizes. One of them alone contains 30,000 idols, most of which are rude images carved out of solid blocks of wood and heavily gilded. They are about three feet high, and some possess many arms and hands, symbols of power and plenty. In many of these temples priests are continually writing on slips of paper the prayers of worshippers, who request that these petitions be pinned or pasted up in the sanctuary. In many Japanese shrines there are gongs, which are beaten vigorously by any one who comes to pray, to arouse the attention of the Deities, and notify them of the prayer about to be offered. Bronze bells of great purity of sound are also to be seen there, and they are rung at stated intervals by the priest with a strangely beautiful effect. Kioto has to-day a population of more than 300,000; but it no longer has the proud position it once occupied, when it was the capital of Japan and the sole residence of the Mikados. At present the seat of sovereignty has been transferred to Tokio, and there is now the palace of the Japanese Emperor. Perhaps no country in the world offers so much to interest the thoughtful traveller to-day as does Japan. Intelligent, progressive, assimilating with wonderful rapidity the ideas, customs and inventions of European and American civilization, the Japanese are, nevertheless, a race having a national record and a regular succession of Mikados for more than 2,000 years. In them the past and present strangely meet and blend. The interesting question is, out of this union what future is to be evolved?

HARBOUR OF RIO JANEIRO, BRAZIL.—Who has not heard of the glorious harbour of Rio Janeiro, the principal seaport of South America? No matter how experienced the traveller may be who enters this commodious and lovely sheet of water, he at once acknowledges that it is unsurpassed by any harbour in the world. The entrance to it is between two steep hills, each more than 1,000 feet in height. The space between them is only 1,700 yards wide, and at the base of each hill is a fort. Beyond that narrow portal, however, there are *fifty square miles of anchorage*. This bay has a width varying from two to seven miles, and extends inland from the ocean for sixteen miles. Its coast line, without counting minor irregularities, measures sixty miles. Moreover, all around this land-locked harbour are picturesque mountains and beautifully rounded hills of varied forms, largely covered with luxuriant vegetation. Upon the bosom of this bay of Rio are many islands, varying in size from some which are six miles long and have a population of 2,500 people, down to little islets having only a few dwellings. Near the city itself there are extensive dock-yards, where most of the Brazilian cruisers have been built. Here, too, is the Naval Arsenal of the country. As might be supposed, the coasting and foreign trading here is enormous, and the harbour of Rio always presents a very animated and pleasing appearance, for merchant vessels, steamers and war-ships from all quarters of the globe are often congregated here in great numbers.

THE CATHEDRAL, CITY OF MEXICO.—The Mexican Cathedral is the most imposing structure in the city. Its corner stone was laid in 1573, and the building covers the site of the great Aztec temple destroyed by the Spaniards when they captured the Capital of the Montezumas in 1521. The entire cost of this Cathedral was about £400,000. The great bell, nineteen feet high, in one of its towers, alone cost £2,000. It is built of stone and its dimensions are impressive, the length of the edifice being nearly four hundred feet, and the towers two hundred and three feet in altitude. The interior, though grand from its magnitude, is somewhat disappointing. Its wooden floor is hardly worthy of so prominent a shrine as this, and the decorations are neither tasteful nor comparable to those of the notable European cathedrals. An enormous amount of money, however, has been expended here. Its high altar is said to have once been the richest in the world, but has been repeatedly plundered of its treasures. A balustrade of great value still surrounds the choir. Some of its chapels have fine paintings, but one can hardly appreciate them in the dim light which only partially reveals their beauty. Here are buried many of the old Spanish Viceroys, as well as the first Emperor of Mexico, Augustin Iturbide. In front of this cathedral is the Plaza Mayor, the great square of the city, which always presents a very animated appearance, and quite near the sacred edifice is the attractive flower-market where Indian women offer superb bouquets of flowers for a mere trifle.

CHINATOWN, SAN FRANCISCO.—"*A trip to Chinatown*" is an essential feature of a visit to the Pacific coast, and a memorable experience it often proves to be. Within a limited area in San Francisco in which 3,000 Europeans would be cramped for room, are always living at least 20,000 Chinamen, whose one idea seems to be to hoard up all the money they can possibly obtain, in order to return in a few years to their native land. It is a most repulsive and apparently dangerous quarter of the city, although crimes are said to be of rarer occurrence there than elsewhere. Moreover, whatever may be said of them in other respects, drunkenness is hardly known among the Chinese. They frequently stupefy themselves with opium, but not with rum. The shops in Chinatown are most grotesque, with their (to us) unintelligible decorations and letterings, recalling memories of the fantastic characters displayed on tea-caddies and bunches of fire-crackers. The variety of merchandise in these shops, its comical arrangement, together with the mysterious dark rooms in the rear, presumably the sleeping apartment of some Wee Lung Chin and family, are all most novel and amusing. The names of the merchants here have that curious combination of monotonous monosyllables which causes them to slip from the memory like drops of water from a duck's back. Interspersed with the shops and tenement houses are several Joss-Houses, or Chinese Temples. Here, too, are Chinese Theatres, where the entire audience smokes, and the performance goes on amid a hideous beating of drums and gongs. The gambling dens and opium cellars in Chinatown should be visited in company with a policeman. They are filthy places where either gambling is carried on by a mass of repulsive Chinese, or opium is being smoked by men dozing in a half-drunken sleep.

SANTA LUCIA, NAPLES.—Naples is the noisiest city in the world, and the quay of Santa Lucia is the place where the Neapolitan uproar asserts itself most loudly. Wheels are clattering, whips are cracking, donkeys are braying, minstrels are singing, and men, women and children are screaming, shouting and quarrelling, as if all Bedlam had broken loose. Sound sleep is here impossible. The arms of Morpheus refuse to embrace the ever-noisy Santa Lucia. Crowds listen with delight to men who are often clad in rags, but who repeat whole cantos of Italian poetry with that passionate fervour which makes the Italian a natural actor. Public letter-writers pursue their avocation here for the benefit of those who cannot themselves write. Toilets are also here performed *al fresco*, and hair-dressing is an invariable feature of most of the doorways. Naples has been truly described as a "Paradise inhabited by devils;" but they are such amusing, merry devils that one does not altogether object to the pandemonium which its streets present. "Santa Lucia! Santa Lucia!"—These are the dulcet words which echo in our ears from dawn to dusk and dusk to dawn. For the name of this wave-washed quay has become the burden of the most popular song in Italy, and "Santa Lucia" floats ever on the air of Naples. How a photographer ever contrived to represent this street as tranquil and deserted as it here appears, is difficult to imagine, unless he chose for the experiment the noontide hour of a broiling summer day.

THE PETROWSKI PALACE, MOSCOW, RUSSIA.—A little outside of the city limits is this famous Palace, built by the Empress Elizabeth more than a century ago, but now used freely as a pleasure-resort by many of the Muscovites, who come here in crowds to attend the little summer theatre in the garden, to drink tea in the open air, and to amuse themselves socially in the long lovely summer evenings, which are so characteristic of these Northern lands, and which in some degree atone for their lack of daylight in the winters. This Palace is historically interesting from the fact that Napoleon took refuge here in 1812 from the flames and fire-brands of burning Moscow. One seems to see here, therefore, now at every turn the face of the amazed and disappointed Emperor, already half anticipating his disastrous retreat, and seeing in that lurid glare of Russia's burning capital an obscuration of his star of Destiny. To the Russians the great disasters of the French in 1812 seem the result of a direct intervention of Providence in their behalf, and the most magnificent church in Moscow, the Cathedral of the Saviour, was erected in gratitude for those events. But at present the Russians who assemble in the grounds of the Petrowski Palace cherish no hard feelings against the French, and certainly the French cheer and admire everything that is Russian. Bygones have become bygones, and the two nations are apparently united in a lasting friendship.

BATTLE OF RIVOLI, GALLERY OF BATTLES, VERSAILLES.—One of the finest paintings in this Martial gallery is that entitled the Battle of Rivoli. It is the work of the celebrated artist Phillipoteaux. It represents the young Napoleon at one of the proudest moments in his eventful life, as he conducted that memorable struggle amid the Alps in 1797, when he so signally defeated the Austrians. The portrait of Bonaparte is admirable. He seems inspired.   Genius is visible in every line of that thin, pale face.   In fact nowhere was his stupendous military genius more discernible than on the plains of Lombardy and in the gorges of the Italian Alps, where the "Little Corsican" with but a handful of ill-fed, ragged troops again and again defeated the proudest armies of Austria and her most experienced generals.   "Do *experienced* generals oppose me ? " cried the young commander ; "So much the better ! I will soon make them burn their books on tactics and know not what to do."   In fact his wonderful rapidity and power of instantaneous decision gave him the speed and spring of a lion. "The French do not *march*," exclaimed an Austrian officer, "they *fly !* " The story of Bonaparte's victories in Italy, of which this of Rivoli was one of the most brilliant, reads like a romance.   It was never equalled even by himself, save possibly in 1813 when the Emperor, ruined by the Russian campaign, was struggling single-handed against united Europe.   But in Italy in 1797 Fortune was with him.   In France in 1813 he had tempted the fickle goddess too far and his star was waning, to sink at last behind the wave-washed rock of St. Helena.

PANORAMA OF SEVILLE FROM THE GIRALDA, SPAIN.—From the summit of the old Moorish spire, the Giralda, the view of Seville is one of exquisite beauty. Clasping it in beauty, like a silver girdle, is that stately river, whose Moorish name (the Guadalquiver) sounds, even when pronounced in English, like a strain of music. It is a very ancient city, famous for distinguished men, lovely women, palm-trees and orange-groves, charming courtyards, fine churches, and many rare paintings by Murillo and Velasquez. From Seville two of the most celebrated and admirable Roman Emperors, Hadrian and Trajan, went forth to wear the imperial purple of the world. Here the gifted Moors reigned for many centuries in splendour. The promenade of Seville discloses a multitude of bewitching Senoras and Senoritas, who wrap around their handsome tresses lace mantillas, which, when adorned with a red rose or a pink, are certainly the most becoming and coquettish head-dresses in the world. Each house in Seville, however plain its exterior may be, will have its pretty courtyard paved with marble and enclosed by walls enamelled with glazed tiles. In these charming patios occur in the soft delightful evenings of Seville the little informal social parties, which render a residence here agreeable. A few modern squares are to be found here, but it is often unpleasant to cross their broad expanse of fiery sunlight, and the narrow, Moorish streets, into which the sun only fully enters for an hour at noon, seem better suited to its climate.

GOVERNMENT HOUSE, CALCUTTA, INDIA.—Calcutta is the capital of British India, and the Government house, the residence of the Queen's Viceroy there, is a most imposing structure. It is of great size and is built around a spacious and beautiful garden. But its massive walls remind us that it could be utilized as a fortress, did necessity require. From this Government building an immense esplanade, called the Maidan, extends for two or three miles along the river, forming not merely a grand parade-ground for military displays but a delightful promenade for all foreign residents in the cool of the evening, when the sun, the tyrant of the day, has disappeared, and its terrific heat has been succeeded by comparative coolness. The climate of Calcutta is so trying that for nearly half the year the Viceroy and as many of his officials as can escape, leave the Government house and flee to the first range of the Himalayas, twelve hundred miles away! For in the hot season in Calcutta the mercury sometimes rises to 120 degrees in the shade, and to 170 degrees in the sun! Most English residents in India have to send their children home when they are five or six years old, as by that time they usually begin to droop and pine away. Even removing them to the mountains then has no effect. Nothing but a return to England will save them. This city of nearly a million inhabitants presents of course the widest extremes of wealth and poverty; for nowhere is such a difference more marked than in half-civilized lands. It is not merely the English with their brilliant uniforms and carriages, who stand in striking contrast here to the wretched natives, but Indian Princes themselves still live in something of their former extravagance, which hints to us still of Oriental luxury.

NASSICK, INDIA.—Nassick is one of the most sacred of Hindoo towns. Thirteen hundred families of Brahmin priests are established here and form a population by themselves. Through this city flows the sacred river Godavari, second in sanctity only to the Ganges itself. All noble Hindoo families keep special "family priests" here to perform devotions for the household and to represent them, as it were, continually at the sacred shrines. The river is lined with many temples, like the one displayed in this illustration, and in their vicinity may be sometimes seen hundreds of men, women and children bathing in the hallowed waters of the Godavari. In close proximity to these temples are little booths, where idols are sold. One can not travel anywhere in India without perceiving the tremendous influence which its varied religions exert upon its millions of inhabitants. Temples, idols, shrines, pilgrims, sacred streams, religious festivals attended by hundreds of thousands of people, all these impress themselves continually upon the retina and on the mind. Some temples there are actually sacred to animals; for in the eyes of the Hindoos all life is sacred, and it seems to many of them a crime to ill-treat or to kill even insects and reptiles. There is, not far from Nassick, a Hospital for animals, where sick or wounded dogs, cats, rabbits, monkeys and birds are protected and even carefully nursed until they recover or die. If it be superstition which prompts such treatment of those poor, dumb creatures, a little of it in the Occident would do no harm.

CLIVE STREET, CALCUTTA.—This street in India's great political and commercial capital is named after Lord Clive, who played such a prominent part in the subjugation of India and in the establishment here of English power. Thanks to such men as Clive, backed by the boundless wealth of England and her gallant army, Her Majesty, Victoria, as the "Empress of India," now rules this gigantic land from sea to sea. Whatever the world may think of her right to do so, it must acknowledge that she does it well, and that the present condition of India is vastly better than when under the domination of the old native tyrants of the country. For European civilization is immeasurably to be preferred to Asiatic despotism, relieved as the latter was in India by some attractive features. This broad and shadeless street seems unsuited to a climate so unbearably hot, and to a sun so deadly, as those of Calcutta. But at least the heads of most of the people are protected by white turbans, their bodies even are robed in white, and the tops of the carriages are painted white in order not to attract any more than is necessary the fierce solar rays. Some buildings thoroughly European in appearance are seen in almost every prominent street in Calcutta, but the influence of Hindooism makes itself felt here despite all these English surroundings, and bodies are cremated and thrown into the river at Calcutta almost as freely as at Benares, and temples here are visited by troops of pilgrims. One of the deities worshipped in this city is the Goddess Kali, who has in fact given her name to the place itself; for Calcutta is only an English pronunciation of Kali-ghat.

EXCURSION BOATS ON THE NILE, EGYPT.—There are two modes of travel open now to the voyager on the Nile. One is the steamboat journey, which is expeditious, comfortable and comparatively inexpensive. The other is a voyage on one of the Dahabeeahs, or private boats, represented in this illustration. Where time and money are of no special consideration, the Dahabeeah is of course much to be preferred. One is thus absolutely independent of the time-table; he can linger as long as he likes at certain points, and he can choose his own companions—a most important matter where one must otherwise travel for weeks with strangers under very peculiar circumstances and in a very limited area. The traveller who hires at Cairo one of these boats, together with its crew, is for the time the master of a floating castle, and if his Dragoman be a reliable one, and his subordinates honest and obedient, it is almost impossible to imagine a more delightful way in which to spend weeks and even months than on the surface of this majestic river, in the most delicious of climates, untroubled by a drop of rain, and surrounded by the grandest ruins of antiquity. The busy and exciting Western World is left behind and almost forgotten, as we glide day after day along this old historic avenue of Egypt, which leads us back amid stupendous temples through the mirage of memory and imagination to the great dawn of human history.

YEZO MEN, JAPAN.—The island of Yezo is the most northern portion of Japan and is largely inhabited by a race of men who are the descendants of the ancient Aborigines of the country. No mention of Yezo is made in the early historical records of the Japanese, and it was perhaps unknown to them until the last of the Ainos (the original inhabitants of Japan) were expelled from the Main Island. The difference between the Japanese and the "Yezo Men" is still plainly visible, especially in the amount of hair which grows on the bodies of these dwellers in the North, in contrast to the Japanese, who are among the least hirsute of any people on the globe. The climate of Yezo is quite cold. For six months it is more or less covered with snow. Much of the interior still consists of primeval forests, rarely penetrated except by these descendants of the Ainos in quest of bears and other wild animals. There are few good roads in Yezo and most journeys must be made there on horseback. There is, however, regular communication by steamers between certain points of Yezo and the Main Island of Japan. This northern region is not without many natural features of great beauty. Its coast scenery is very fine, its lakes and mountains offer a pleasing variety, and one or two moderately active volcanoes serve to relieve life of complete monotony. The "Yezo Men" in the civilized parts of the island are by no means savages. As this illustration shows us, they are respectably clothed, their dwellings are well thatched, and their fences are at least substantial if not graceful. Their boats, too, though primitive, are skilfully fashioned, and under the manipulation of these stalwart natives, they cleave the water with great speed.

THE CITADEL, CAIRO, EGYPT.—Far above most of the mosques and dwellings of Egypt's fascinating capital is a massive fortress built in 1166 on a hill commanding a magnificent view not only of the entire city, but of the Nile, the Desert, the Pyramids and the Sphinx. It was largely constructed out of stones taken from some of the Pyramids. Close by it is the "Alabaster Mosque" of Mahomet Ali, the founder of the present Egyptian dynasty. Its well-proportioned domes rest lightly one upon another, like beautifully rounded clouds, while its slender marble minarets rise into the blue air, looking, when tinged with the glow of sunrise or sunset, like silver lances tipped with points of gold. Gloomy memories haunt that Cairene citadel. There in 1811 occurred the massacre of the Mamelukes by order of Mahomet Ali, who wished to be rid of these political enemies. He invited them to a banquet in that fortress, and they came, magnificently attired, to the number of 470 men. Hardly had they entered the courtyard of the citadel, when the gates were closed behind them, and a murderous fire was opened on them by the Viceroy's troops, who suddenly appeared upon the walls. Unable alike to defend themselves or to escape, they fell in one red, writhing mass, with the exception of one man, who, spurring his horse over the weltering bodies of his comrades, forced him to leap on and over the parapet to the plain below. It was a fearful distance. One moment he was in mid-air; the next he was freeing himself from his mangled steed amid a shower of bullets. Yet he escaped, as if by miracle, into the adjacent desert, the only one preserved of all that brilliant band.

THE CAPITOL, ROME.—In the very heart of the Eternal City is a majestic flight of steps crowned at the summit by colossal statues of Old Roman Gods found in the baths of Diocletian. It was down the steps which these have now replaced that Rienzi, "last of the Roman Tribunes," fled in his last moments, to fall at their base, bleeding from twenty wounds; while from a window in their palace burning on the hill, his beautiful young wife looked down and saw his tragic death. In the square at the summit of this staircase is the place where Brutus harangued the unwilling populace after the murder of Cæsar. There stands to-day the famous bronze equestrian statue of the Emperor Marcus Aurelius, the only perfect equestrian figure which has come down to us of all that once adorned Imperial Rome. Hawthorne, as all will recollect, describes this beautifully in his romance of the "Marble Faun." That statue (the Faun of Praxiteles) is one of the treasures of the Art Museum of the Capitol, which contains also the "Dying Gladiator," the "Capitoline Venus," and many other celebrated statues of antiquity. There too are many busts and statues of the Roman Emperors and their families; and perhaps no part of Rome is better adapted to contain the portrait-gallery of its ancient rulers than this Capitoline hill, the scene of many of its earliest glories and its latest crimes.

MOSQUE OF SULTAN ACHMET, CONSTANTINOPLE, TURKEY.—One of the grandest Mosques in Constantinople is this, erected about 1615 A. D. by Sultan Achmet. It is the only Mosque in the world which has six minarets, all the others having usually two or four. These minarets are of great beauty, being entirely composed of pure white marble, and encircled with several finely sculptured balconies which appear to the fancy at a distance like jewelled rings betrothing earth and heaven. These minarets are not intended merely for ornament. They are continually used. Five times a day, punctual as a figure moved by clock-work, on every such minaret in the city appears the Muezzin, or Mohammedan caller to prayer. He chants out upon the air the sacred formula of Islam: "God is great. There is but one God. Mahomet is the Prophet of God. Come to prayer." Towards the four points of the compass are these words directed; then all is still, save the echo of some more distant voice. This Mosque is the scene of the grandest ceremonies of Islam, and also of many of the Court processions. The Sultan often comes here on State occasions attended by his entire suite, particularly at the festival of the Prophet's birth. Then the Sultan and all the members of his Court appear in great splendour. The interior of this Mosque is magnificently decorated with lofty columns, exquisite mosaics and a handsome marble pulpit. On one side of this sacred edifice is a balcony, where all the Sultan's decrees ("Firmans") are read aloud. All Mosques in Stamboul have some remarkable attractions, peculiar to themselves, but none is on the whole more interesting than this Imperial gift of Sultan Achmet.

LA GUAIRA, VENEZUELA.—Venezuela is a portion of South America to which more and more travellers are resorting every winter. A line of steamers run regularly from New York to La Guaira, which is the principal sea-port of the Republic. It is interesting to remember that the coast of Venezuela was the first part of the American mainland sighted by Columbus, when, during his third voyage in 1498, he sailed along a portion of the Orinoco river. In the following year a much greater extent of the country was discovered by other navigators, among whom was the celebrated Amerigo Vespucci, whose name was given to both the Northern and Southern continents. La Guaira is a place of great activity. Situated on the Caribbean Sea, it is only five miles from Caraccas, of which it is the port. It has practically only two streets, extending east and west, and occupies a narrow strip of land between the mountains and the sea. Although it is the most frequented sea-port on the coast, nevertheless, when ships have unloaded their cargoes at La Guaira, they often go on further to secure safer anchorage. The climate of La Guaira is considered healthy (for Venezuela), as yellow fever is not so prevalent there as in many other places on the shore; but the heat is excessive, the mercury frequently ranging from 100 to 110 degrees Fahrenheit. The principal export of La Guaira is coffee, and in respect to the *quantity* of coffee shipped to foreign lands Venezuela ranks fifth among the coffee-producing countries of the world.

GUANAJUATO, MEXICO.—Guanajuato is a capital of a State of the same name, 238 miles north of the City of Mexico. Its name is said to have been derived from an Indian word meaning "The Hill of the Frog," and was so called because a huge stone in the shape of a frog was once worshipped here. At present the divinity most worshipped at Guanajuato is the Almighty Dollar, though it must be said that Guanajuato is not unique in this particular! It is a marvellously productive mining town. One of its mines is said to have produced £160,000,000! Its annual silver product now is about £1,200,000. It is built in a deep and narrow ravine, along the sides of which the buildings cling in such odd positions that an earthquake shock would apparently send them all tumbling down in great confusion. Silver was discovered here in 1548, and since then the tawny, desolate mountains which enclose this town have proved a treasure-house of wealth. One sees, however, few indications of such riches in the town itself. The streets are narrow, roughly paved and filled with disagreeable odours. The buildings, with the exception of a few houses in the upper part of the city, are as plain as though the adjacent hills were mounds of sand, instead of silver, and the poor Indians look as usual ragged and wretched. Great floods sometimes occur here occasioning loss of life and property. Some handsome churches, the Citadel, the Mint, and the Silver Mills, reward the traveller's visit to this place, aside from the picturesque and mediæval features of the town itself.

THRONE-ROOM, BUCKINGHAM PALACE, LONDON.—"A throne," said Napoleon, "is only a collection of boards covered with velvet." Nevertheless, it symbolizes so much of wealth, rank and power, that one approaches it with at least respectful interest. The Throne-Room of Buckingham Palace, the usual London residence of Queen Victoria and her household, is a magnificent apartment. Its length is sixty-four feet. Its walls are covered with crimson satin. The royal chair itself stands on a slightly elevated platform beneath a velvet canopy. This is, however, by no means the only room within this palace which repays the traveller's inspection. The Ball Room, the Banquet Hall, and Picture Gallery, the various Reception Rooms and, above all, the splendid staircase of the palace, which together with its elegant Corinthian columns is of pure white marble; all these are what we might expect in this abode of English royalty. The interior of Buckingham Palace is, however, much more attractive than its exterior, although adjoining it is the extensive palace-garden, which contains sixty acres, and is very beautifully kept, and possesses a pretty summer house, frescoed by such distinguished artists as Maclise and Landseer. This little villa has been used by Her Majesty when she has been obliged to spend any of the summer season in the city. Near this palace are the Royal stables, where are kept the state carriages and the horses of the Queen.

PENNSYLVANIA AVENUE, WASHINGTON, D. C.—Washington, like Paris, is a city of noble perspectives. Its stately avenues, smoothly paved with asphalt, are not merely handsome thoroughfares in themselves; they have also at their termini either buildings of superb proportions or groups of statuary commemorating many of the statesmen and generals of the nation. Pennsylvania Avenue is the most prominent of all Washington's streets. That part of it which connects the Treasury and the White House with the Capitol is straight as an arrow, is about a mile and a quarter long, and has a width of 160 feet. If the structures which front upon it were only of a uniform height, the appearance of this famous avenue would rival that of almost any in the world. Unfortunately too much individual irregularity is permitted in the architectural embellishment of American cities, and while a certain amount of variety is always desirable, glaring contrasts in style and above all in height, detract from an otherwise beautiful effect. Upon this avenue, or very near it, are many of the leading stores, hotels and theatres. At one extremity rises, like a snow-covered mountain, the dome of the Capitol; at the other is the truly majestic building of the Treasury. This city is appropriately named after the nation's first President, for it was Washington himself who chose its site, and who laid the corner-stone of the Capitol in September, 1792. Seven years later the seat of the Government was removed thither from Philadelphia. The city was also planned and laid out by Andrew Ellicott under Washington's supervision. The latter desired to have it called "Federal City," but his own name was bestowed on it, and it was incorporated as a city on the 3d of May, 1802. In 1860 its population was 60,000. In 1890 it was 230,392.

WASHINGTON ELM AND MEMORIAL STONE, CAMBRIDGE, MASS.—The suburbs of Boston are remarkably beautiful. To drive through them almost anywhere within twenty miles of the city is like riding through a park adorned with villas and rural palaces. One of the suburbs, Cambridge, is attractive not merely from its shaded streets and elegant residences; it wears the classic air of a University town, since here is located "Fair Harvard," whose various edifices, embowered in the shadows of majestic elms, possess remarkable architectural beauty. Almost within a stone's throw of the University, in the centre of a broad, old-fashioned street, is an aged tree, before which stands a granite tablet. On this in gilded letters is an inscription telling us that beneath this tree Washington took command of the American army on July 3d, 1775, at the commencement of that struggle of the colonies for independence which was only won after such a terrible struggle—a struggle which drenched the land with the best blood of the mother country and of the children who were striving to rid themselves of the ties that bound them to her. America is but a young nation even now; but the past century has been so wonderfully eventful that it is hard to realise that only a hundred and seventeen years have passed since this old tree spread its canopy of shade above that memorable scene—a scene whose memories have been happily obliterated for Englishmen by a century of friendship.

LONGFELLOW'S HOUSE, CAMBRIDGE, MASS.—One of the most interesting sights of this classic town is the home of the poet Longfellow. It is a spacious, old-fashioned "Colonial" mansion, painted in yellow and white, and situated on a grassy terrace. On the right and left of the pathway leading to it are lilac bushes which fill the summer air with perfume, while a graceful elm casts on the lawn beneath a tremulous mosaic of light and shade. The room in the right hand lower corner of this fine old structure was the poet's study. From its windows there is a pleasant view of Charles river (the "Silent River" of his verse), together with the undulating hills of Brookline and Brighton. This study contained many interesting memorials of literary men, which Longfellow highly prized. Such were the inkstand of Coleridge, the waste-paper basket used by Tom Moore, and the chair given to the poet by the children of Cambridge. Longfellow bought this house in 1837, and here, "beneath the elm-trees' nodding crest," he wrote all his poems from 1837 to 1845, including his famous "Psalm of Life," which was composed in 1838. Here too he wrote "Hyperion," and here in his darkened study, when suffering from trouble with his eyes, he traced out in pencil the lines of "Evangeline," which next day would be copied off and read to him for his corrections. This home of Longfellow has an interesting history. It was built in 1759 by Col. John Vassall, who abandoned it when he left for England on the eve of the Revolution. As it was confiscated to the State, Washington took it for his headquarters when he came to Cambridge to assume command of the American army. Here almost all distinguished visitors to America have been entertained. Within this house in 1861 the poet's wife met with the terrible accident which caused her death, and here twenty years later Longfellow himself passed away from earth, esteemed and beloved by the whole English-speaking world.

INDEPENDENCE HALL, PHILADELPHIA.—Plain and old-fashioned among many new and imposing edifices, like a modest Quaker dress amid the fashionable toilets of a ball-room, stands the historic structure known as Independence Hall. Here we may see the very room in which the Continental Congress met, and where, on the Fourth of July, 1776, the Declaration of Independence was adopted, signed and proclaimed to the people gathered in the adjoining square. The walls of this room are lined with portraits of many of the patriotic signers of that Declaration, and there are still preserved the table and many of the chairs used by the Deputies. Opposite this is another room of equal size filled with most interesting souvenirs of those heroic days. Among these are articles of furniture used by Washington, La Fayette, Benjamin Franklin and John Hancock. Letters, swords, articles of wearing apparel, and authentic portraits also vividly recall to us the patriots who were not found wanting "in the times that tried men's souls." There also is the heavy framework on which the famous "Liberty Bell" was originally hung, and in the corridor of the building one may still see the historic bell itself now cracked and voiceless, but eloquent in the memories which it awakens of the days when, first of all the bells in the United States, its tones rang out in joyous peals, announcing the adoption of the Declaration, and proclaiming "Liberty throughout the land to all the inhabitants thereof." In "Congress Hall," an apartment in the second story of this building, Washington delivered his farewell address.

THE OLD CITY GATE, ST. AUGUSTINE, FLORIDA.—The Spaniards who established themselves in St. Augustine under Menendez in 1565, more than half a century before the "Mayflower" brought the Pilgrims into Plymouth Harbour, left many traces of their conquest. They built, among other works, a massive wall across the entire peninsula, from shore to shore, to protect the city on the north. The greater part of this has long since crumbled to decay, or been removed for building purposes. One fragment of it still remains, however. It is this "City Gate," situated now at the head of St. George Street. As we look upon its old square towers, containing loop-holes for the guns of sentinels, our thoughts are inevitably carried back to the time when this, the oldest European settlement in the United States, was a point of danger. Few places in America have been more frequently the scene of desperate conflict. Fierce Indian tribes for years kept its inhabitants in constant apprehension. French soldiers, too, have more than once attacked it. It was twice assailed by expeditions from the neighbouring English colonies of South Carolina and Georgia. It has been held in turn by many masters. Spain, England, Spain again, and finally the United States, have one by one possessed it, and during the war between the North and South it changed masters three times. Souvenirs of these memorable events abound in and about St. Augustine. In one place, for example, is a monument erected in 1812 to commemorate the Spanish Constitution. The United States Barracks here formed once a monastery for Franciscan monks. While the fine old fortification called Fort Marion is an interesting relic of the past, which was 100 years in building, and has its gateway still ornamented with the arms of Spain, carved in the massive stone. The purpose of the people of St. Augustine to-day, however, is not to repel the outside world with ponderous battlements or walls, but rather to invite them to come in and revel in its lovely scenery and balmy climate: for its immense hotels are able to receive an army of invading tourists.

THE ALCAZAR AND CORDOVA, PONCE DE LEON, ST. AUGUSTINE, FLORIDA.—St. Augustine is probably the oldest European settlement in the United States.   More than fifty years before the Pilgrims landed on the "stern and rock-bound coast" of Massachusetts, the Spaniards had taken possession of the place.   It was even ceded by England back to Spain in 1783, and only came into the possession of the United States in 1819.   Quiet enough in summer, in winter it becomes a very popular and fashionable resort, receiving usually about 10,000 visitors during "the season."   To accommodate this multitude of tourists, enormous hotels have been constructed here.   This illustration shows two of them, the "Alcazar" and the "Cordova," as they appear to one looking from the "Ponce de Leon."   These buildings are remarkable in many ways.   The Ponce de Leon hotel covers four acres of ground and is a half-mile in circuit !   Not only has it spacious dining-rooms, an immense rotunda and the like, but it contains billiard-rooms for ladies, an enormous play-room for children, and even studios for artists.   The Hotel Cordova has a "sun-parlour" 108 feet long and paved with tiles.   The architecture of St. Augustine is a charming mixture of old Spanish residences with hanging balconies along their second stories, and beautiful American villas of the kind which make Nahant and Newport so attractive.   The streets of St. Augustine are extremely narrow, frequently only ten or fifteen feet in breadth.   This gives to the town a pleasant flavour of the Orient, for in every land of the sun narrow, shaded streets are a luxury always to be appreciated. Most of the Spanish houses, as well as the old Spanish Fort of San Marco near by, are made of a conglomerate of fine shells and sand.   There are charming drives about St. Augustine, and a delightful promenade a mile in length extends along the great "Sea Wall."   The climate here in winter is mild, yet not enervating, and oranges, lemons, bananas, figs, palms and all sorts of tropical plants grow here in profusion.

CAÑON DE LAS ANIMAS, COLORADO.—Europe has at least no monopoly of grand natural scenery, which is scattered broadcast in the New World. One special feature of it is magnificently displayed in Colorado, which is par excellence the land of cañons. What fjords are to Norway, cañons are to Colorado—enormous wrinkles in the face of Mother Earth, huge mountain corridors through which an ancient Scandinavian would have said the Gods strode downward to the plains. One of the grandest of these Colorado cañons is that displayed in this illustration, not far from the mining town of Silverton. On either hand tower these almost perpendicular cliffs with hardly a scrap of vegetation on their barren sides, leaving between them barely space enough for the crystalline river, which writhes and struggles with obstructing boulders, lashing itself to creamy foam and fills the chasm with a deafening uproar. One can hardly imagine a more exciting journey than that which is afforded by the railway train, which with sublime audacity climbs upward on its grooves of steel and follows all the windings of the stream shut in by massive walls upon a shelf of rock hundreds of feet above the foaming torrent, which is both glorious and terrible to look upon. It is an awe-inspiring place, for miles without a sign of life, weird, solitary and sublime with its vast treeless summits and its jagged cliffs. Well did the Spaniards call this mountain stream "El Rio de las Animas Perdidas" (the "River of Lost Souls"); for such a gorge as this appears a fitting entrance to the infernal regions, and on these dark precipitous rocks might be appropriately inscribed the words which Dante saw above the door of Hell, "All hope abandon ye who enter here."

WINDY POINT, PIKE'S PEAK, COLORADO.—One by one the great mountains, whose snow-white summits once seemed destined to remain ever virgin to the foot of man, have yielded to their conqueror. Mt. Blanc, the Jungfrau, and even the Matterhorn, have now been climbed so frequently that half the charm and mystery which once surrounded them like sun-lit clouds has been dispelled. On some of these great ice-clad sentinels actual fetters have been placed, and cog-wheel railways scale their jagged rocks, and make them as accessible to tourists as a caged lion of the desert is to visitors to a menagerie. One of these vanquished mountains thus enchained is Pike's Peak in Colorado. It was no easy task to subjugate it. It has a height of 14,300 feet. Its cliffs are wild and savage in appearance. Its summit is perpetually white with snow. Yet now a railway transports travellers to its crest from Manitou in an hour and a half and the "Great Snow Mountain," as Major Pike called it in 1806, can now be ascended and descended in a few hours! Across this "Windy Point" the wind sweeps often with tremendous violence, for Pike's Peak stands in a peculiarly exposed position on the edge of the vast Colorado mountain chain. Yet on the summit of this mountain is a station of the Weather-Signal Bureau, which is occupied winter and summer. Eight thousand feet below this is the pretty little city of Colorado Springs, so justly famous for its wonderfully pure air and delightful climate. The drive from this city to Manitou, five miles nearer to Pike's Peak, is one of great beauty, and commands magnificent views of the mountains, Glen Eyrie, and the "Garden of the Gods."

CLIFF DWELLINGS, MANCOS CAÑON, ARIZONA.—From time immemorial men have chosen their places of residence from a desire to defend themselves from invasion. Actuated by such motives, the pre-historic Lake Dwellers of Switzerland built their huts on piles driven into the bed of Lake Lucerne. The Aztecs chose the site of Mexico for similar reasons. Almost all the great cities of antiquity, from Jerusalem to Toledo, were found in localities which could be easily defended. This same instinct of self-defence is seen among the Aborigines of America, and particularly in the strange Cliff Dwellings which we find in Arizona, Colorado and New Mexico. In some instances the cliffs at a height of forty or fifty feet above a river have been worn by flood and tempests into grooves, crevices or shelves, usually from four to six feet wide. On these rude structures have been built. Their walls are sometimes eight or ten inches thick, the stones being laid in mortar. One group of such dwellings is 800 feet above the river. The only way of reaching some of these houses, even when one has climbed to the rocky shelf, is to go through the foremost structures. Those in the rear were formerly impregnable, even if the others should be taken. To reach some apartments in these Cliff Dwellings, a man would have to enter an aperture only twenty-two inches high and thirty wide, and crawl through a tube-like passage twenty feet in length! Some can be reached only by ladders to the second story, the lower story being solid without any opening. The former Cliff Dwellers were probably related to the Pueblo Indians. Some of these structures were still inhabited when the Spaniards invaded this region. Cliff Dwellings are known to have existed also in Central America three centuries ago.

SHOSHONE FALLS, IDAHO.—The Snake river in Idaho, like most of the streams in the mountainous regions of the Northwest, has an adventurous career. The fall before us is the most conspicuous of its cataracts, and forms, in its descent, a beautiful curve, resembling a Moorish arch. Ages ago Nature, as if to test the strength of this wild mountain torrent, erected here a barrier to its course. It was in vain. With a shout of triumph in its leap for liberty, the river bounds over this obstacle, falls seventy or eighty feet, extricates itself from the seething depths below amid great mounds of spray which sparkle in the sun like clouds of diamonds, and sweeps along unharmed and free. There has evidently been a struggle here in ages past. These grim and splintered rocks, rising above the waters, look like some scarred and mutilated veterans, who thus far have survived the combat, while the forms of their companions have been buried in the flood below. Yet our sympathy is not with them. It is rather with this freedom-seeking river, which will not bear resistance, but which attacks and overleaps its enemy with a roar of defiance that can be heard for miles. Twenty or thirty years from now, when all this wonderful section of the country shall have become widely known, and suitable hotels and roads can make a tour here delightful, it will be found that here are waterfalls surpassing many of the famous cataracts of Europe, which nevertheless are now almost without a name, and certainly without renown.

THE GRAND CAÑON, YELLOWSTONE NATIONAL PARK. —Of all the marvels of the Yellowstone National Park, the most sublime is the Grand Cañon. Through this the Yellowstone river, which is a tributary of the Missouri, flows in one place for twenty continuous miles between perpendicular cliffs only about 200 yards apart and from 1,200 to 1,500 feet in height! At the entrance to this part of the Cañon the whole river makes a stupendous leap of 360 feet, in what are known as the "Lower Falls." The sides of this gigantic chasm have literally almost all the colours of the rainbow displayed upon their vertical surfaces. Red, orange, yellow, green, blue, violet and white tints are constantly succeeding one another here in wonderful variety, thus lighting up with glory countless architectural forms, which Nature, it would seem, had fashioned here to make the proudest works of man appear diminutive and tame. These colours doubtless have been formed by the percolating through the cliffs of the hot mineral waters from the neighbouring springs. Distinguished painters have sadly declared that any adequate representation of these brilliant, variegated hues is utterly beyond the power of human art. What an unrivalled combination is there, therefore, in this Cañon, of awe-inspiring grandeur and enchanting beauty! And what a magnificent pathway has been given to the Yellowstone river! Leaving the famous Yellowstone lake enclosed by snow-clad mountains, it passes through a series of rapids and a fall of 140 feet before it even reaches the Grand Cañon, and just beyond this it receives a tributary which in its haste to join it makes a leap of 156 feet! Thus cradled in sublimity, the Yellowstone river must be called in some respects the most extraordinary stream even in the American continent.

CRATER OF THE GIANT GEYSER, YELLOWSTONE NATIONAL PARK.—The surface of this globe which we inhabit, compared with its diameter, is only about the thickness of the rind of an orange in proportion to its entire mass. Beyond a certain depth the earth's temperature rapidly increases on account of the great heat of its interior. Wherever the crust on which we dwell is especially thin or weak, a portion of our planet's pent-up energies bursts forth in the form of volcanoes, geysers, hot springs, or earthquakes. That wonderful region reserved by the American Government as a "National Park" is particularly remarkable for the number and size of its geysers. Volcanic action here has evidently held high carnival in pre-historic ages, and remnants of its furious outbursts are still seen in the almost innumerable masses of steam and water ejected from its area. Some of these geysers hurl into the air rocks and boulders as well as water, the latter rising sometimes to a height of 200 feet. The temperature of the water is usually more than 170 degrees. One of these geysers, called "Old Faithful," spouts regularly every hour throwing the water to the altitude of 130 feet, and holding it up by a succession of impulses for about five minutes. Another maintains its immense uplifted volume of boiling water for twenty minutes! The "Giant Geyser" has a rugged crater (outlined in this illustration), about ten feet in height and twenty-five in diameter. This is one of the most irregular of all the volcanic fountains here. It has been known to spout continuously for three and a half hours, its height varying from 90 to 200 feet.

MOUNT HOOD, OREGON.—Among the snow-crowned monarchs of the "New Northwest" one of the most imposing is Mt. Hood. Its height is 11,570 feet, but it appears even greater because of its fine conical form, piercing the azure in the likeness of a pyramid of silver. Around its base are miles of gloomy forests, from which this mountain rises heavenward in its robe of purity, as some celestial visitor might withdraw from the dark, evil passions of mankind. As these trees reach the flanks of the great mountain, they strikingly resemble the advance-guard of a mighty army, which can go no further towards scaling the gigantic fortress above them, apparently half granite and half crystal. There has evidently been a conflict here between the forces of Life and of Death; and as the snow-line comes in sight Death creates fearful havoc in the ranks of the invaders. Many of these trees are twisted and broken by wind and avalanche, and everywhere we see the bleached and mouldering forms of those which have succumbed to winter's cold. Mount Hood is beautiful at any time, but never is it so wonderfully impressive as when the full-orbed moon rises above this sea of giant pines to pour an added flood of silver over its mantle of eternal snow. At such a time, when Mount Hood cuts its dazzling silhouette against the dark blue sky, one can imagine it a mighty iceberg drifting in crystal splendour from the Polar Sea.

THE THREE SISTERS, CANMORE, CANADIAN PACIFIC RAILWAY.—The scenery along the Canadian Pacific line is, at certain points, magnificent. Snow-covered mountains, deep ravines, sparkling cascades and lovely valleys succeed each other, mile after mile and hour after hour, in the neighbourhood of the Rocky Mountains. At Canmore an observation car is attached to every train to permit the passengers to enjoy an unbroken view of the varied and imposing panorama visible on either side. A prominent feature of it is that group of mountains known as the Three Sisters, beyond which other peaks arise, like suitors, to attend them. It is impossible for photographic art to give any adequate idea of the scenery on this splendid route to the Pacific. Sometimes so narrow is the gorge that no possible outlet is discernible; but in a moment more an unexpected turn or gloomy tunnel transports the long-drawn, swiftly moving retinue of human lives into some new and still more glorious surroundings. From valleys beautifully fresh and green rise countless mountains 9,000 or 10,000 feet in height, their sides and summits silver-white with snow, rolling away, one peak beyond another, to meet the sky, as crested waves might look to occupants of a little boat tossed in the hollows of a stormy sea. The forms of these wild mountains also offer infinite variety; being at times pyramidal, at other times resembling castles with projecting towers, or huge cathedrals with their flying buttresses and slender spires; while glittering glaciers, too, occasionally reveal themselves like jewelled highways of the Gods.

ROYAL GORGE, COLORADO.—Sometimes the walls of one of the wild gorges rise perpendicularly from the water's edge, leaving no space for a man to walk beside the foaming stream of which it is the passage-way. At other times the cañon widens into a narrow valley, through which roads are made. Some gorges are hemmed in by walls 300 or 400 feet in height, while others are enclosed by cliffs 1,000 or 1,200 feet in altitude. The Grand Cañon is even 4,000 feet in depth! In some the swiftness of the current equals that of the "Flying Dutchman"; in others it descends with moderation and is fairly navigable. Some have their walls of marble carved by the elements and polished by the waves, and glittering with almost all the colours of the rainbow. All sorts of architectural forms have shaped themselves on either side in ages of the past, till now their awe-inspiring buttresses and pinnacles look like the ruined and deserted castles of the Gods. No photographic view can ever do such scenery justice, nor can the most brilliant writer give to it sufficient praise. The pencil of Gustave Doré alone might partially reveal the weird and awful grandeur of these Colorado chasms, hundreds of miles in length, thousands of feet in depth; terrific scars upon the face of Mother Earth, which never more shall be effaced until our Planet's cycle of existence shall have brought it once more to its Parent Sun

EL CAPITAN, YOSEMITE VALLEY, CALIFORNIA.—This sublime feature of the Yosemite Valley is not so high as some of its adjoining mountains, but from the peculiar position which it occupies it has received deservedly the Spanish title given to it, "El Capitan," or "*The Commander*" of the valley. Professor Whitney declares that it is doubtful if anywhere in the world there is presented "so squarely-cut, so lofty and so imposing a face of rock." It projects into the valley as a promontory advances into the sea. It is 3,300 feet high, and its walls are almost perpendicular, without a scrap of vegetation on their surfaces. Opposite this is the lovely "Bridal-Veil Fall," which plunges over a stupendous cliff, and long before it reaches the earth is converted into a mass of silvery spray, tinted at times with all the colours of the rainbow. How strange it seems now to reflect that not until 1851 had a white man ever gazed upon the natural wonders of this valley! For years it had been the almost inaccessible hiding-place of savages, as well as the abode of wild beasts. The latter fact is evident from its Indian name, Yosemite, which signifies "Great Grizzly Bear." What a title to bestow upon this most magnificent valley! Yet we may well retain the musical Indian appellation while forgetting its meaning.

"WAWONA" BIG TREE, MARIPOSA GROVE, CALIFORNIA.—Who has not heard of the "Big Trees," of California? They are another proof of the fact that the western portion of America is a region marvellously endowed by Nature. There are in the area here which has been set aside by Congress "for public use, resort and recreation," more than 600 trees, which have in respect to size no rivals in the world. A stage-coach, with driver, passengers and horses can be driven through the upright hollow trunk of one of these forest giants, which nevertheless is still sufficiently alive to bear leaves on its branches *300 feet above the ground!* Even more enormous than those still flourishing here are some prostrate monsters, one of which must have had a circumference of 120 feet and a height of 400 ! The largest tree now standing here has a circumference of about 100 feet and its first branch (six feet in diameter) is 200 feet from the ground ! It is an extraordinary fact that the cones of these trees are no larger than walnuts, and their seeds are only about a quarter of an inch in length. One feels himself a pigmy as he stands beside these forest Titans, not only in comparison with their prodigious size, but as he measures his brief life with the long line of thirteen centuries, of whose slow march their annual rings and weird colossal limbs give proof.